DISCOVERING THE BIBLE

IN THE NON-BIBLICAL WORLD

The Bible & Liberation

An Orbis Series in Biblical Studies

Norman K. Gottwald and Richard A. Horsley,
General Editors

The Bible & Liberation Series focuses on the emerging range of political, social, and contextual hermeneutics that are changing the face of biblical interpretation today. It brings to light the social struggles behind the biblical texts. At the same time it explores the ways that a "liberated Bible" may offer resources in the contemporary struggle for a more human world.

Already published:

The Bible and Liberation: Political and Social Hermeneutics (Revised edition), Norman K. Gottwald and Richard A. Horsley, Editors

Josiah's Passover: Sociology and the Liberating Bible, Shigeyuki Nakanose

The Psalms: Songs of Tragedy, Hope, and Justice, J. David Pleins

Women and Jesus in Mark: A Japanese Feminist Perspective, Hisako Kinukawa

Liberating Paul: The Justice of God and the Politics of the Apostle, Neil Elliott

Becoming Children of God, Wes Howard-Brook

Biblical Hermeneutics of Liberation: Modes of Reading the Bible in the South African Context, Gerald West

The Bible & Liberation Series

DISCOVERING THE BIBLE
IN THE NON-BIBLICAL WORLD

Kwok Pui-lan

ORBIS BOOKS

Maryknoll, New York 10545

Copyright ©1995 by Kwok Pui-lan

Grateful acknowledgment is made to the following for permission to reprint from previously published material:

Christian Conference of Asia for "Women and the Ministry of Jesus," which was published in *Peoples of Asia, People of God: A Report of the Asia Mission Conference, 1989* (Osaka: CCA, 1990), 109-18.

The Crossroad Publishing Company, New York, for "Racism and Ethnocentrism in Feminist Biblical Interpretation," which was published in *Searching the Scriptures*, Vol. I: *A Feminist Introduction*, edited by Elisabeth Schüssler Fiorenza (New York: Crossroad, 1993), 101-16.

Scholars Press for "Discovering the Bible in the Non-Biblical World," *Semeia* 47 (1989): 25-42.

Stony Point Center (Stony Point, N.Y.) for "The Promised Land: Biblical Reflection in a Time of Sorrow," *Centering* (Spring/Summer 1992): 7-9.

Published by Orbis Books, Maryknoll, NY 10545-0308
Manufactured in the United States of America

Library of Congress Cataloging-in-Publication Data

Kwok, Pui-lan.
    Discovering the Bible in the non-biblical world / Kwok Pui-lan.
        p.   cm. — (Bible & liberation series)
    Includes bibliographical references (p.) and index.
    ISBN 0-88344-997-8
    1. Bible—Feminist criticism—Asia.   2. Bible—Feminist criticism—
Developing countries.   3. Feminist theology—Asia.   4. Christianity
and culture.   I. Title.   II. Series.
BS521.4.K96   1995
220.6'082—dc20   95-10028
                                                                        CIP

To
The Rev. Canon Hwang Hsien-yuin,
one of the two women officially ordained
in the Anglican Communion,
November 28, 1971

Contents

PROLOGUE

(I presented the following Bible study in dramatized form at the Asian Mission Conference, organized by the Christian Conference of Asia in Indonesia in 1989. I dressed first in an Indian sari to portray Mary, the mother of Jesus, then in an Indonesian batik to depict the three women who questioned Jesus' identity, and finally in white linen to symbolize the women in the passion story.)

When women study the Bible, we do not read from a written text. Instead, we share our stories, songs, and dreams. We sing, we dramatize, and we wait for the presence of the Holy Spirit. This morning I want to invite you to look at the Bible from a woman's perspective.

I believe the way we interpret the Bible is conditioned and influenced by our backgrounds. I come to you as a Chinese, deeply moved by recent happenings in China and impressed by the thousands of Chinese students who have given up their lives for democracy. I come to you as a woman, mother of an eight-year-old daughter, who has listened to Asian women's stories, shared their pain, and rejoiced in their hope. I come to you as a Christian theologian, having received years of theological training yet refusing to follow the western male style of doing theology.

At this conference we are trying to reflect on God's mission among the suffering and struggling peoples of Asia. I want to share with you how I, as a Chinese woman theologian, reread the gospel story in light of the recent historical crisis of my people. I ask you to listen, not only with your ears, but also with your hearts in order to discern what the gospel event means for us today.

THE CHINESE CRISIS

Blessed are the blind,
for they do not have to see.
Blessed are the deaf,
for they do not have to hear.
Blessed are the numb,
for they do not have to feel.
But they cannot stop their hearts

> from pulsating with the hearts of children at
>   Tiananmen.
> But they cannot stop their hearts
> from pulsating with the hearts of children at
>   Tiananmen
> except those who are dead.[1]

This is part of a poem written by a Beijing citizen on June 5, 1989, the day after the Chinese People's Liberation Army marched into Tiananmen Square in Beijing, crushing the students with army tanks and firing at them with machine guns.

In mid-April of that year, the sudden death of the former Communist Party Secretary Hu Yaobang gave rise to a series of memorial services and meetings in China. Students in Beijing soon turned these commemorative ceremonies into public protests against government corruption, the lack of freedom of expression, and the suppression of human rights. When the government condemned such activities as illegal and counterrevolutionary, about two thousand college students decided to go on a hunger strike in protest. On May 17 people from all walks of life, including workers, journalists, teachers, and doctors, declared their support of the peaceful student demonstration, and more than one million people gathered in a mass rally. A few days later, popular demonstrations of comparable size took place also in Shanghai, Shenyang, and other Chinese cities. In addition, in both Taiwan and Hong Kong, more than one million people took to the streets in support of the Beijing students and their struggle for democracy.

Chinese political leaders were divided in their views of how to deal with a popular demonstration of such magnitude, one that threatened the legitimacy and power of the Communist regime. The diehard leftists opted to crush the "insurrection" with military force, but the liberals hoped to solve the confrontation through negotiation and peaceful means. Unfortunately, the leftists gained the upper hand, and the People's Liberation Army was ordered to enter Beijing city on May 22. As the army marched into the city, it was prevented on several occasions from advancing on Tiananmen Square by students and local residents. In the end, at midnight of June 4, the army encircled the square and fired at the crowd with machine guns. By dawn, Tiananmen Square was a bloodbath and a living hell.

We do not know the exact number of casualties, since the Chinese government continues to lie, saying that the army did not fire at the students at all. But according to the estimates of eyewitnesses and international reporters, between two and three thousand young people were killed during the incident.

> Blessed are the deaf,
> for they do not have to hear the screams.
> Blessed are the blind,

for they do not have to see the tanks
trample on the students.

The events unfolding in Beijing had tremendous impact on the Christian community, both in China and in Hong Kong. Christians are still in the process of reflecting on the theological significance of this unprecedented, large-scale demonstration for democracy. What does the Gospel have to say to such an historical crisis? Who is Jesus for the suffering and struggling peoples of Asia? How did Jesus understand his Jewish identity and express his patriotism? As a woman, I am particularly interested in the roles women played in the ministry of Jesus.

JESUS BORN OF MARY

According to the Bible, Jesus' mother was Mary, a simple and humble Jewish woman. As a young maiden, Mary was, at first, not sure of her mission and the prospect of having a child before marriage. Like other anxious young mothers, she went to seek help from her women friends. When she came to visit Elizabeth, she found both support and reassurance.

As Jane Chui of Hong Kong has pointed out, Mary had a tremendous sense of the historical destiny of her people.[2] She saw the child in her womb as a promise of God and a blessing to Israel:

> My soul magnifies the Lord,
> and my spirit rejoices in God my Savior,
> for he has looked with favor on the lowliness of his
>   servant.
> Surely, from now on all generations will call me
>   blessed.
> . . . .
> he has filled the hungry with good things,
> and sent the rich away empty.
> He has helped his servant Israel,
> in remembrance of his mercy,
> according to the promise he made to our ancestors,
> to Abraham and to his descendants forever.
> (Luke 1:46-55)

With the help of Joseph, Mary raised her son Jesus within the Jewish tradition. Together they brought Jesus to Jerusalem to keep the Jewish Passover, and Mary accompanied Jesus to a Jewish wedding at Cana.

Jesus respected his parents and loved his mother, and he extended this love and regard to women around him in saying, "My mother and my brothers are those who hear the word of God and do it" (Luke 8:21).

JESUS AND HIS JEWISH IDENTITY

When Jesus went through the villages preaching the Gospel, there were women included in the *ochlos*, that is, the crowd of people following him. Among them were women whom Jesus had healed of evil spirits and illnesses, such as Mary Magdalene, Joanna, the wife of Herod's steward, Susanna, and many others; these women provided food and other necessities for Jesus and the disciples (Luke 8:1-3). The Jewish women in the villages of Galilee heard the rumor that a young man had come forth preaching good news that they had never heard before. He spoke of a new kingdom of God, challenging the existing order and its authorities. Most important of all, he said that women, just like men, would have an important place in this kingdom.

One woman reportedly heard Jesus saying, "The kingdom of heaven is like yeast that a woman took and mixed in with three measures of flour until all of it was leavened" (Matt. 13:33). Another reported that Jesus even spoke of the kingdom as like a woman searching for a lost coin. When she finds it, she will call her friends and neighbors to rejoice with her. Jesus said when one sinner repents, the angels will rejoice in the same way as the woman does (Luke 15:8-10).

The women also heard Jesus debate vigorously with their teachers, the Pharisees and the scribes, concerning many aspects of Jewish tradition and Law. Jesus challenged their views on marriage and divorce, on adultery, and on prostitution. Was Jesus not a Jew? Was he not a man of Nazareth? Did he not understand the importance of Jewish tradition for his people under the yoke of Roman rule? How dare he call the Pharisees and scribes hypocrites!

In fact, Jesus' identity and his patriotism were repeatedly challenged by the women he met during his ministry. When Jesus passed through Samaria, he met a Samaritan woman at the well and discussed with her the proper place of worship. Jesus told her, "Woman, believe me, the hour is coming when you will worship the Father neither on this mountain nor in Jerusalem. You worship what you do not know; we worship what we know, for salvation is from the Jews. But the hour is coming, and is now here, when the true worshipers will worship the Father in spirit and truth" (John 4:21-23). Although Jesus clearly appreciated the significance of Jerusalem for the Jewish community, he refused to limit the presence of the almighty God to the Jewish Temple.

In carrying God's mission into Asia, we keep hearing people asking these questions: Where is God? Is God to be found in the Church or among the people? Where is the spirit? Is the spirit bestowed upon Christians only, or is the spirit found also among people of other faiths? We recall that Jesus did not ask the Samaritan woman to go to the Temple in Jerusalem. Instead he said the true worshipers would worship in spirit and truth.

Similarly, after the June 4 massacre, many Chinese Christians learned that God's action cannot be restricted to the Church alone. Some Christian leaders pointed out that the Beijing incident shows that God does not always act through the Church. In the past, we have often assumed that God's revelation is in the Church, and through the Church to the world. But the sacrifice of the students in Beijing teaches the Church that God is active in the world. Christians have to discern God's work among the people.

In another incident Jesus was confronted in the Temple with a prostitute caught in adultery (John 8:1-11). The scribes and the Pharisees meant to use the occasion to trap Jesus. They asked him, "Now in the law Moses commanded us to stone such women. Now what do you say?" Jesus' fidelity to the Law was at stake. He bent down and wrote with his finger on the ground, pondering how to respond. Finally he stood up and said, "Let anyone among you who is without sin be the first to throw a stone at her." While the scribes and the Pharisees were concerned about how to keep the tradition and the Law, Jesus was probably wondering what was the use of the Law when it could not even protect a downtrodden woman.

In this particular story the sexually abused body of the woman becomes a powerful symbol of injustice in society: the oppression of the rich against the poor, the powerful against the powerless, men against women. Today the suffering of prostitutes in large Asian cities such as Hong Kong, Jakarta, Bangkok, Manila, and Seoul, of female laborers working long hours in multinational corporations, and of peasant women on the Asian subcontinent and in other rural areas challenges the hypocrisy of the so-called miracles of economic development. Their bodies cry aloud, decrying the "collective sin" of our Asian society.

Likewise, the dead bodies of the Beijing students call into question the legitimacy of Chinese traditions and law. In fact, the peaceful demonstration of the students was preceded by a serious reconsideration of the Chinese cultural tradition and political situation by intellectuals in Beijing. They began to ask important questions regarding the essence of Chinese culture, the process of modernization, the need for democratization, and the future of socialism. When the Chinese government officials charged that the students' demonstration was a conspiracy against the Communist Party and a denial of socialism, the students asked what was the use of "ideologies" and "isms" when people suffered from soaring inflation, government corruption, and social instability. Like Jesus, they questioned the legitimacy of a law and a social order that ignored human suffering and disregarded people's dignity. They challenge us to look for a vision of a new society where people will be able to live in peace and justice, and where there will be true partnership between women and men.

Jesus' identity and concern for his own people were challenged a third time by a Canaanite woman in the district of Tyre and Sidon (Matt. 15:21-28). This woman begged Jesus, "Have mercy on me, Lord, Son of David; my daughter is tormented by a demon." Jesus revealed a deep patriotism when he replied, "I was sent only to the lost sheep of the house of Israel." Further, when the woman came to kneel before him, he was not moved: "It is not fair to take the children's food and throw it to the dogs." Yet, her persistence prevailed, so that Jesus finally promised, "Woman, great is your faith! Let it be done for you as you wish."

God's salvation is not limited to the Jews, nor to the Canaanites, nor to any particular people. Asian people suffer under the yoke of economic oppression, military dictatorship, totalitarianism, and patriarchal cultural tradition. Like the little daughter of the Canaanite woman, many are possessed by the power of a demon. Yet the quest for freedom and human dignity has become the common aspiration of all oppressed people, regardless of race, color, or nationality. As the Beijing students say, "Democracy is the noblest sentiment of human existence, and freedom is the natural right of human beings."[3] We have to identify with people's pleas and bring the suffering to partake in God's salvation. The Canaanite woman challenges us to have faith in God and to be in solidarity with the people. Her ministry to the little ones possessed by the power of a demon shows us what it means to be a Church of the people.

WOMEN AND THE PASSION OF JESUS

Jesus' iconoclastic understanding of the Temple, the Law, and God's salvation brought him into direct confrontation with the existing authorities. When he decided to go to Jerusalem, his followers knew that something important and dramatic was about to happen. Jesus predicted that there would be war, violence, and instability, realities that many Asian people know firsthand.

Entering the Temple, Jesus could not control his passion for Jerusalem and her people: "Jerusalem, Jerusalem, the city that kills the prophets and stones those who are sent to it! How often have I desired to gather your children together as a hen gathers her brood under her wings" (Matt. 23:37). The women following Jesus would understand instantly what Jesus meant, and their hearts would resonate with Jesus' anguish and compassion.

In fact, it was a woman who first recognized that Jesus' mission was soon to be fulfilled. This woman came to Jesus with an expensive ointment and poured it over his head. Jesus was so impressed by her faith that he said, "Wherever this good news is proclaimed in the whole world, what she has done will be told in remembrance of her" (Matt. 26:13).

During the Last Supper the women were busy preparing the meal, but even in the kitchen they could overhear Jesus saying that somebody would die and there would be bloodshed. Was Jesus planning a revolution? Why did someone have to die? Perhaps Jesus told them something similar to what the Beijing students wrote before their hunger strike:

We do not want to die; we want to live, because we are in the golden period of our youth. . . . But if the death of one person, or a group of persons, can make the lives of people better and the motherland more prosperous, we do not have the right to live.[4]

In Gethsemane, Jesus went to pray alone to God: "My Father, if it is possible, let this cup pass from me; yet not what I want but what you want" (Matt. 27:39). The night when the Beijing students knew that the army would soon march in, they also wondered if they could stand up to the test, but they entrusted their lives to the cause of the people.

Finally, the soldiers arrived. They came to capture Jesus. They came to fire at the students. Thousands of Beijing citizens came out to stop the tanks, saying, "The people's army should not fire at the people."

When the soldiers got hold of Jesus and started torturing him, his disciples fled, knowing that repression would follow. Jesus' mother, like all the mothers of political prisoners, could hardly hold back her tears, worrying about the life of her child. The mothers of the college students in Beijing said, "Children, we wish to keep you at home. Do not go to Tiananmen Square. Yet we understand that you must go."

Jesus was hanged on the cross and suffered a torturous death. But just before his last breath, he comforted his mother, entrusting her to his beloved disciple. As the students in Beijing were preparing to die for their country and people, the following song became very popular:

> Perhaps I have to bid farewell,
> and return no more.
> Do you understand? Do you comprehend?
> Perhaps I will fall down,
> and rise up no more.
> Will you wait for me forever?
> If this is so, don't be sorrowful.
> The flag of the Republic,
> will have our blood-tainted countenance.
>
> Perhaps my pair of eyes
> will open no more.
> Do you understand
> my passion deep and silent?
> Perhaps I will sleep,
> and rise up no more.
> Won't you believe I will change into mountains?
> If this is so, don't be sorrowful.
> The soil of the Republic,
> will have my sacrificial love.[5]

After Jesus died, his followers would not dare to come near for fear of persecution. They were afraid that the government would try every means to identify them and put them on trial too. Only the women whom Jesus loved gathered together to prepare the tortured body for a proper burial. Toward the dawn of the first day of the week Jesus appeared to the women and told them to weep no more. Mary Magdalene and the other Mary were to be the first witnesses of the risen Christ before the whole world.

Even today, people are still debating whether the women indeed saw the risen Christ or just a ghost. But the women at the tomb and the countless other women who had been healed by Jesus, heard his preaching, and been moved by his passion knew that they had a story to tell. Just as the students in Beijing continue to sing:

> There is a dragon in the ancient East;
> its name is called China.
> There is a people in the ancient East;
> they are all descendants of the dragon.
> Under the dragon's feet we grow,
> growing up to be the descendants of the dragon,
> black eyes, black hair, and yellow skin
> forever and ever the descendants of the dragon.[6]

I ask you to join with me to observe a moment of silence for the students in China, Korea, and other Asian countries who have given up their lives for their country, and for all others who have died for freedom and democracy.

INTRODUCTION

This book is an attempt to dialogue with the Bible from multiple perspectives as an Asian woman theologian. The journey of writing this book began several years ago when Katie Geneva Cannon and Elisabeth Schüssler Fiorenza invited me to contribute an article for an issue of *Semeia*.[1] In that article I criticized the ethnocentric use of the Bible in the colonial contexts, and I articulated a new model for interpretation based on the reading of the Bible by Asian theologians. After that volume was published, I was glad to see that other contributors were struggling likewise to create an alternative interpretive space, one that was not defined by Euro-American biblical scholarship.

My article, "Discovering the Bible in the Non-Biblical World," contributed to the emerging biblical scholarship of Third World[2] women and has been reprinted in different anthologies.[3] Continuing the critical task I have begun, I use the title of that article for this book. It may be worthwhile to explain why I chose that eye-catching title for *Semeia*. At first, I had thought of something like "Liberating the Bible for the Non-Christian World," intending to challenge the parochialism of Euro-American biblical scholarship for failing to take significant notice of the global context in which we live. But on second thought, I realized that a reactive mode would not particularly help channel my energy into articulating something different and new.

While I was looking for a better expression, Paul A. Cohen's important book *Discovering History in China* came to mind. In that book Cohen analyzes the different paradigms in American scholarship for studying modern Chinese history. Noting that western scholars have often used a western-centered approach to study Chinese history, Cohen urges his colleagues to adopt a China-centered paradigm. Cohen uses the term *discovering* to signify the move from an external perspective toward a more internal approach, one that sees the history of a given non-western society in its own terms and from its own point of view rather than as an extension of western history.[4] Similarly, Asian Christians must discover the Bible from perspectives that emerge out of their own contexts, and not through a western lens.

The Bible is chosen as the focal point of my study for several reasons. First, the Bible has a very controversial, ambivalent, and often conflicting status in Asia. During the nineteenth century the Bible was introduced to many parts of Asia as an integral part of the colonial discourse. It has been used to legitimate an ethnocentric belief in the inferiority of the Asian peoples and the deficiency of Asian cultures. But the same Bible has also been a resource

1

for Christians struggling against oppression in Asia, especially in the Philippines and South Korea. Second, in Asia the Bible encounters a wholly new cultural context, one with a long hermeneutical tradition that challenges the hegemony of western models of interpretation. Third, many new paradigms for biblical interpretation have emerged in the past several decades, creating more space in which to raise new questions and to use one's creativity and imagination. With new insights from the social sciences and cultural and literary studies, our understanding of the relationship among the text, the context, and the reader becomes much more diverse and sophisticated.

For me, Asia is the non-biblical world. Asian peoples comprise 56 percent of the world's population, while the percentage of the Christians in Asia is less than 3 percent. Compared to Latin America, where Christians are the majority, and Africa, where Christians constitute about 28 percent of the population,[5] the percentage of Christians in Asia is extremely small. Despite centuries of missionary effort, Asian people have persistently rejected the Bible and Christianity. The intricate link between Christianity and colonialism is a contributing cause. Other factors include the vitality of ancient historical religious traditions, the difficulty of translating Christian concepts in a cross-cultural context, and the different relationship between religion and society. In the past the Bible has been used by Christians as the norm by which to judge other cultures. The time has come for us to listen to the questions and challenges posed by the people whose lives and cultures are not shaped by the biblical vision.

A critical examination of the Bible and its interpretation is important for Asian Christian women. Asian feminist theology emerged as a movement of Bible study at the grassroots level. Christian women gathering together to read the Bible raised questions based on their life experiences and searched for a more liberating hermeneutics. In the past decade different networks of Asian women have published several anthologies focusing on the Bible. Women in the Christian Conference of Asia published *Reading the Bible as Asian Women* in 1986.[6] The Asian Women's Resource Center for Culture and Theology published *Women of Courage* in 1992[7] and the center's journal, *In God's Image*, carries many interesting essays on reading the Bible through Asian eyes. Documenting the discussion on the Bible and Asians' struggle, the Asia-Pacific office of the World Student Christian Federation published in 1992 *Re-Living Our Faith Today*.[8] Asian female members of the Ecumenical Association of Third World Theologians met in 1989 and 1990 to search for Asian feminist hermeneutical principles, and one of the papers has been published.[9]

Since there are few academically trained biblical scholars in Asia, many Asian women writers have to rely on biblical and theological scholarship by western women. The pioneering works of Elisabeth Schüssler Fiorenza, Phyllis Trible, and Rosemary Radford Ruether are often quoted.[10] My earlier publications on the Bible were influenced by these scholars, because they have interpreted the Bible from feminist viewpoints.[11] But I have begun to see that

Asian Christian women cannot simply apply western biblical scholarship—as if it were context free—to the Asian situation. Many Asian women theologians who cautiously avoid borrowing indiscriminately from western feminist theology are not so self-conscious in using feminist biblical scholarship. We are generally more aware of the contextual nature of theology, while believing biblical scholarship to be objective and scientific. There is the assumption that Asian women can analyze our socio-political situation, whereas western feminist scholars can tell us what the Bible means, and that the two sides can be easily correlated. This position fails to take into consideration the hermeneutical principle that what we see depends on where we stand. Western feminist scholars insist that there is no "objective" or "value-neutral" interpretation of scripture, and such critical insight is equally applicable to their own work. Since they write for an audience with a drastically different context, they fail to touch on many hermeneutical issues that face Asian Christian women.

The aim of this book is precisely to ask these questions. It is an exploratory attempt, an initial test of the field, and a preliminary mapping of the territory. It does not try to provide all the answers, which will come only after a more in-depth digging of the historical and textual sites, the creation of more non-Eurocentric models for cross-cultural comparison, the collective critique of established biblical criticisms, and the creative articulation of new hermeneutical paradigms. This is clearly beyond the effort of a single scholar; the task requires sustained discussion within the Asian theological community and beyond.

In the research and writing of this book I find myself constantly pressing on the boundaries of the fields of the history of religions, hermeneutics, and biblical and theological studies. I have to go back to the fundamental question of how I look at the Bible and at my own interpretative project. Do I see the Bible as a classic or as scripture? Am I a cultural critic, a hermeneutician, a theologian, or all of these?[12] Raised in the Asian context, such questions have different connotations and entail a different configuration of issues from those in the West. We may have to reconceptualize the notion of "scripture," examine anew the relation between Gospel and culture, and explore further the relationship between biblical scholarship and Asian feminist theology.

I have found that a rigid separation of disciplines and a superficial delineation of the East and the West are not helpful for my work. From my teacher Benjamin I. Schwartz, I have learned that cultures are not isolated and impermeable, and that a clear boundary that defines East and West, or North and South, does not exist. It is the "subtle, nuanced difference in between," or the gray area of "fruitful ambiguity" that offers new opportunities for critical scholarship.[13] While this book focuses on Asian interpretation of the Bible, the issues it raises are not unique to Asia. I certainly hope that the book will be of help to biblical scholars and theologians from other contexts.

From another vantage point I recognize that intellectual relationship with the West is very complex in postcolonial Asia, involving not only appropriation but also resistance. Having grown up in Hong Kong, I have intimate knowledge of what living as a colonized people means. Before 1971 English was the only official language in Hong Kong. My parents' generation, mostly refugees from China, had to rely on somebody else to read an official letter, to file a tax form, and to understand government notices. The experience has heightened my consciousness of Eurocentric hegemony and the colonization of the mind. While I have borrowed insights from the critical theory of Foucault, Derrida, and Lyotard, I use them discriminately to debunk the totalizing discourse of the West, without indulging in their Eurocentric systems of thought. Similarly, when using the theories of non-Europeans, such as Edward W. Said and Gayatri Chakravorty Spivak, I appropriate them in the context of critical biblical interpretation in Asia.

Discovering the Bible in the Non-Biblical World is divided into seven chapters. The first three chapters set the historical and theological contexts for approaching the Bible from the perspective of Asian women. The next four chapters examine four sets of issues in Asian feminist hermeneutics: orality and textuality in biblical interpretation; multifaith hermeneutics; postcolonial criticism; and racism and ethnocentrism in feminist biblical interpretation. The chapters do not progress in a linear or sequential manner. The thought processes behind the writing is multidimensional and correlative in nature, instead of linear, monolithic, and deductive. Each chapter represents one of multiple entries to the subject and a proliferation of possible lines of growth.[14] While each chapter has its own internal coherence, together they form a pattern, a configuration, and a structure for seeing the whole. The Prologue and the Epilogue, presenting two concrete examples of my own practice of biblical interpretation, frame the whole discussion and add narrative diversity as well as a more personal voice to the book.

Chapter 1 is a slight revision of my article in *Semeia*. With the help of Foucault and Derrida, I attempt to destabilize the authority and the universal truth-claims of the Bible in the colonial discourse. Through analyzing reflections on the Bible by Asian authors, I propose "dialogical imagination" as a new approach to biblical interpretation. Such an approach uses Asian myths, legends, and stories as the context for biblical reflection, and the social biography of Asian people as a hermeneutical key to understand the Bible and Asian reality. I also present my own critical reflection on the text, the canon of the Bible, and the norm of interpretation.

Chapter 2 deals with the relationship among the Bible, the critic, and the theologian in the pluralistic Asian context. Instead of using the Bible as the norm for other scriptures, it places the Bible within the larger, multiscriptural context of Asia and argues for a more fluid, dynamic, and relational understanding of scripture. Analyzing the multilayered identity of an Asian critic, it evaluates the usefulness of western models of criticism as applied to Asia. The need to derive hermeneutical principles and methods of interpretation from Asian cultural and religious traditions is emphasized. Finally, the complex issue of how to use the Bible in feminist theology is discussed.

In Chapter 3 the relationship among language, thought, and knowledge from the Chinese context is analyzed and its implication for hermeneutics clarified. Drawing from cultural resources from China and the theory of language by M. M. Bakhtin, I articulate more carefully the presuppositions for a dialogical model of interpretation. After discussing several images and metaphors of the Bible offered by various theologians, I offer an image of the Bible as a "talking book," inviting polyphonic theological discourses and ongoing dialogues, to conceptualize the pluralistic use of the Bible in Asia.

Chapter 4 discusses the importance of oral transmission in the Asian religious traditions and its impact on biblical interpretation. When I wrote the first chapter several years ago, I was not sufficiently aware that dialogue took different media: the oral and the written. The work of Renita J. Weems has drawn my attention to the poignancy of aural hermeneutics in the African American tradition, and Joanna Dewey has helped me understand the importance of the oral medium in the first two centuries of Christian history. Several examples of oral hermeneutics at work in the Bible studies of Asian women are analyzed to illustrate the creative retelling of familiar stories and the dialogic interaction with the Bible.

While the oral medium is important for religious transmission in Asia, Asia is unique in the Third World in that it has the long hermeneutical tradition of its ancient scriptures. For millennia Asian scholars have produced exegeses, glossaries, and commentaries on the *Book of Change*, the *Dao de jing*, and the *Bhagavad Gita*, to name but a few. Situating the Bible within this long hermeneutical tradition, Chapter 5 discusses the Bible and interfaith dialogue, and critical issues in cross-cultural, multifaith hermeneutics.

Chapter 6 attempts to articulate a postcolonial criticism for Asia. Since the Bible was used as an instrument of oppression in the colonial discourse, Asian theologians must be careful not to reinscribe the unequal power relations in the text. Using the story of the Syrophoenician woman (Mark 7: 24-30) as an example, the chapter analyzes western interpretations of that text and the challenges posed by Asian critics. Building on the work of Gayatri Chakravorty Spivak, several issues in postcolonial biblical criticism are discussed.

The last chapter examines racism and ethnocentrism in feminist biblical interpretation. I try to look beyond Asia and situate the discussion in the wider context of biblical interpretation among Third World, African American, and Asian American women theologians. Ten theses are presented to look at racial and ethnic identity, both in the biblical narrative and in the politics of interpretation. The chapter elucidates how women under multiple oppression can help us rediscover the liberating potential of the biblical message. Written originally for *Searching the Scriptures*, a project commemorating the centenary of Elizabeth Cady Stanton's *The Woman's Bible*,[15] I also intended to remember Zhang Zhujun, known for her preaching from the pulpit at the turn of the century. Doctor Zhang is reportedly the first Chinese woman to have done so.

It is quite obvious that the book deals with a wide range of topics, some of which will require a separate monograph to deal adequately with the challenging issues. I have traveled across disciplines and brought into dialogue authors in different fields who normally do not converse with one another. The image I have is that of the wanderer, as Edward W. Said has described, going from place to place to gather materials, but remaining a person essentially *between* homes. "In the process, what is taken from a place ultimately violates its habitual way of being: there is constant transposition."[16] The wanderer reflects not only the multidimensional thinking process but also my multifaceted identity.

This book presents the journey of discovering the Bible by an Asian woman theologian. I do not claim to speak for or represent other Asians. This disclaimer is necessary not only because Asia is so diverse but also because one's understanding of being *Asian* depends on one's social and historical location. My own background as a Chinese woman, having grown up in the British colony of Hong Kong, carrying a "British Dependent Territories Citizen" passport, belonging to the Anglican church, and having received theological education both in Hong Kong and in the United States points to the complexities in the construction of national, cultural, and ecclesial identities. I have experienced the constant tension of oscillating between different worlds, the freedom to look at one part of myself from another part, and the joy in crossing boundaries and assimilating new insights in a multidimensional way. Currently doing research and teaching theology in Cambridge, Massachusetts, I enjoy many privileges other Asians do not dream of having. At the same time, as a woman and a Chinese in Diaspora, I am twice removed from the center of the American academy and society. I speak from a position of both privilege and marginalization. It is a very limited space, but fluid and creative. I intend to use the relative freedom and privilege I enjoy as strategically as I can to fight the crippling effects of western imperialism and Chinese paternalism at once.[17]

I would like to thank my Asian sisters who over the years have shared their ideas with me and supported my journey: Rose Wu and Lee Ching Chee from Hong Kong, Chung Hyun Kyung and Sun Ai Lee Park from Korea, Virginia Fabella, Mary John Mananzan, and Elizabeth Tapia from the Philippines, Nantawan Boonprasat Lewis from Thailand, Marianne Katoppo from Indonesia, and Aruna Gnanadason from India. I am also grateful to Asian male theologians for their insights and encouragement: C. S. Song, Kosuke Koyama, D. Preman Niles, Yeow Choo Lak, David Kwang-sun Suh, and Kim Yong Bock.

I have benefitted profoundly from conversations with sisters in the Ecumenical Association of Third World Theologians and in the ecumenical movement. I am much indebted to Elisabeth Schüssler Fiorenza for her active interest in my work and for her critical scholarship. Grateful acknowledgment is due to Clarice J. Martin, Renita J. Weems, and Rita Nakashima Brock for making their writings available to me. I am especially thankful to Beverly

Moon, a scholar in comparative religions, for her superb editing and her informed, critical comments. She has insisted that I should not use *fertility cult*, or *animism* without being aware that they have often been used in a pejorative sense. R. S. Sugirtharajah is a source of support and has offered valuable bibliographic assistance. Richard A. Horsley and Satoko Yamaguchi have given helpful feedback on the manuscript. Aina Allen and Miriam Acevedo-Naters have proofread the text with great care. Robert Ellsberg and Susan Perry at Orbis offered much encouragement and convinced me that a book is not the final word but a progress report. My family has constantly stood behind me and provided both time and space for me to concentrate on my work. I am grateful for their companionship and for their patience and understanding. Finally, I thank the Episcopal Divinity School for providing me with support from the Theological Writing Fund.

I have dedicated this book to the Reverend Canon Hwang Hsien-yuin, one of the first two women officially ordained in the Anglican Communion in 1971. She was the vicar of Holy Trinity Church in Hong Kong, which I attended as a teenager. As a strong role model and teacher, she exposed me to a feminist reading of the Bible from early on. The women in my church, some of whom cannot read or write, remind me not to lose sight of the fact that women are not simply passive recipients of the biblical message. As scholars, we have to listen to and learn from them the ways they have appropriated the Bible in their lives.

1

Discovering the Bible
in the Non-Biblical World

"To the African, God speaks as if He [*sic*] were an African; to the Chinese, God speaks as if He [*sic*] were a Chinese. To all men and women, the Word goes out over against their particular existing environment and their several cultural settings." Thus spoke Zhao Zichen, China's best-known Protestant theologian.[1] The central *Problematik* of biblical hermeneutics for Christians living in the "non-Christian" world is how to hear God speaking in a different voice—one other than Hebrew, Greek, German, or English.

Christianity has been brought into interaction with Chinese culture for many centuries, but the Christian population in China has never exceeded 1 percent. Since the nineteenth century the Christian missionary enterprise has often been criticized as being intricately linked to western domination and cultural imperialism. Chinese Christians have been struggling with the question of how to interpret the biblical message to our fellow Chinese, the majority of whom do not share our belief.

In fact, this should not only be a serious concern to the Chinese but a challenge to all Christians with a global awareness, and to biblical scholars in particular. Two-thirds of our world is made up of non-Christians, and most of these peoples are under the yoke of exploitation imposed on them by the privileged one-third. The interpretation of the Bible is not just a religious matter within the Christian community but a matter with significant political implications for other peoples as well. The Bible can be used as an instrument of domination, but it can also be interpreted to work for our liberation.

This chapter attempts to discuss some of the crucial issues that have grown out of the interaction of the Bible with the non-biblical world. I shall first discuss biblical interpretation in the context of the political economy of truth. The second part focuses on biblical interpretation as dialogical imagination based on contemporary reappropriation of the Bible by Asian Christians. Finally, I shall offer my own understanding of the Bible from a Chinese woman's perspective.

BIBLICAL INTERPRETATION AND THE POLITICS OF TRUTH

Biblical interpretation is never simply a religious matter, for the processes of formation, canonization, and transmission of the Bible have always been imbued with the issues of authority and power. French philosopher Michel Foucault helps us to see the complex relationship of truth to power by studying the power mechanisms that govern the production and repression of truth. He calls this the "political economy" of truth:

> Each society has its regime of truth, its "general politics" of truth: that is, the types of discourse which it accepts and makes function as true; the mechanisms and instances which enable one to distinguish true and false statements, the means by which each is sanctioned; the techniques and procedures accorded value in the acquisition of truth; the status of those who are charged with saying what counts as true.[2]

Foucault's analysis leads me to examine the power dynamics underlying such questions as: What is truth? Who owns it? Who has the authority to interpret it? This is particularly illuminating when we try to investigate how the Bible is used in a cross-cultural setting.

Who Owns the Truth?

In the heyday of the missionary movement of the late nineteenth century, John R. Mott, the chief engineer of the campaign that was called the "evangelization of the world in this generation," cried out:

> The need of the non-Christian world is indescribably great. Hundreds of millions are today living in ignorance and darkness, steeped in idolatry, superstition, degradation and corruption. . . . The Scriptures clearly teach that if men are to be saved they must be saved through Christ. He alone can deliver them from the power of sin and its penalty. His death made salvation possible. The Word of God sets forth the conditions of salvation.[3]

Mott and other westerners saw the Bible as the revealed Word of God, which had to be made known to all "heathens," who were by definition living in idolatry and superstition. The Bible served thus as a "signifier" that functioned to support western beliefs in the basic deficiency of "heathen" culture. This western construction was superimposed on other peoples to show western culture as the norm and inherently superior. In a similar way, the phallus has been used as a signifier of the fundamental "deficiency" of the female, a value superimposed on women by men in male psychological discourse.[4] It is not merely a coincidence that missionary literature describes Christian mission as "aggressive work"[5] and western expansion as "intrusion"[6] and "penetration."[7]

The introduction of the Bible into Asia has been marked by difficulty and resistance, mainly because Asian countries have their own religious and cultural systems. The issue of communicating the "Christian message in a non-Christian world" was the primary concern of the World Missionary Conference in 1938. Hendrik Kraemer, the key figure in the conference, acknowledged that non-Christian religions are more than a set of speculative ideas. They are "all-inclusive systems and theories of life, rooted in a religious basis, and therefore at the same time embrace a system of culture and civilization and a definite structure of society and state."[8] Still, his own biblical realism, much influenced by Karl Barth's theology, maintains that the Christian Gospel is the special revelation of God, which implies a discontinuity with all other cultures and a judgment of all other religions.[9]

This narrow interpretation of truth has disturbed many Christians coming out of other cultural contexts. Zhao Zichen, for example, presented a paper on "Revelation" in which he stated: "There has been no time, in other words, when God has not been breaking into our human world; nor is there a place where men [sic] have been that He [sic] has not entered and ruled."[10] Citing the long line of sages, that is, the moral teachers of China, such as Confucius, Mencius, and Mozi, he questioned, "Who can say that these sages have not been truly inspired by the spirit of our God, the God of our Lord Jesus Christ? Who can judge that the Almighty has not appeared to them in His [sic] Holy, loving essence and that they have not been among the pure in heart of whom Jesus speaks?"[11]

In this battle for truth many Chinese Christians have rejected the assumption that the Bible contains all the truth and that the biblical canon is rigidly closed. Already in 1927 Bo Chenguang argued that many Chinese classics, such as the *Analects* of Confucius, the *Mencius*, and the *Book of Songs* are comparable to the books of the prophets, the Psalms, and the Book of Deuteronomy in the Hebrew Scriptures.[12] Since the Bible contains the important classics of the Jewish people that preceded Jesus, he could see no reason why Chinese Christians should not include their own classics as scripture. Others, such as Xie Fuya and Hu Zanyun, argued that the Chinese Bible should include parts of the Hebrew Scriptures, the New Testament, Confucian classics, and even Daoist and Buddhist texts![13] For a long time Chinese Christians have been saying that western people do not own the truth simply because they bring the Bible to us, for truth is to be found in other cultures and religions as well.

Who Interprets the Truth?

Another important question in the political economy of truth concerns who has the power to interpret it. During the pivotal century of missionary expansion, many missionaries acted as though they alone knew what the Bible meant, believing they were closer to the truth. Invariably the gospel message was interpreted to mean the personal salvation of the soul from human sinfulness.

This interpretation reflects an understanding of human nature and destiny steeped in western dualistic thinking. Other cultures, having different linguistic systems and thought forms, may not include similar conceptions. As Wu Yaozhong, a Chinese theologian, notes, "Such terms as original sin, atonement, salvation, the Trinity, the Godhead, the incarnation, may have rich meanings for those who understand their origins and implications, but they are just so much superstition and speculation for the average Chinese."[14]

More important, this simplistic version of the Gospel functions to alienate Christians in the Third World from the struggle against material poverty and other forms of oppression in their society. But in the name of a "universal Gospel," this thin-sliced biblical understanding has been pre-packaged and shipped all over the world. The basic problem of the so-called universal Gospel is that not only does it claim to provide the answer but it defines the question too! American historian William R. Hutchison rightly observes that American missionary ideologies at the turn of the century shared the belief that "Christianity as it existed in the West had a 'right' not only to conquer the world, but to define reality for the peoples of the world."[15] If other people can only define truth according to the western perspective, then christianization really means westernization!

In the 1920s, as a response to the anti-Christian movement, which criticized Christianity as "the running dog of imperialism," Chinese Christians began a conscious effort to define what the Gospel meant for them. Chinese Christians became collectively aware that in their biblical interpretations they had to be accountable to all their fellow Chinese and not just to the tiny Christian minority. For example, they tried to show that the biblical term *agape* was compatible with "benevolence" as defined in Chinese classics. They suggested that the moral teachings of Jesus were comparable to the teachings of the Confucian tradition. As foreign invasion became imminent, the central concern of all Chinese was national salvation, and the gospel message, too, became politicized.[16] In the mid-1930s, anticipating the kind of liberation theology that developed decades later, Wu Yaozhong reinterpreted Jesus as "a revolutionary, the upholder of justice and the challenger of the rights of the oppressed."[17] These attempts at indigenization show clearly that biblical truth cannot be pre-packaged, that it must be found in the actual interaction between text and context in the concrete historical situation.

What Constitutes Truth?

Chinese philosophical tradition is very different from western thought in that it is not interested primarily in metaphysical and epistemological questions. On the contrary, it is more concerned with moral and ethical visions of a good society. The Neo-Confucian tradition, in particular, has emphasized the integral relationship between knowing and doing. Truth is not merely something to be grasped cognitively; it must be practiced and acted out in the self-cultivation of moral beings.

For most Chinese the truth-claim of the Bible cannot be based on its being the revealed Word of God; 99 percent of the people do not believe in this kind of faith statement. They can only judge the meaningfulness of the biblical tradition by looking at how it is acted out in the Christian community. At the time of foreign encroachment in the early twentieth century, Chinese students set forth many burning questions: "Can Christianity save China?" "Why does not God restrain the stronger nations from oppressing the weaker ones?" "Why are the Christian nations of the West so aggressive and cruel?"[18] These probing questions resemble those of Katie Geneva Cannon, an African American ethicist: "Where was the Church and the Christian believers when Black women and Black men, Black boys and Black girls, were being raped, sexually abused, lynched, assassinated, castrated and physically oppressed? What kind of Christianity allowed white Christians to deny basic human rights and simple dignity to Blacks, these same rights which had been given to others without question?"[19]

The politics of truth is not fought on the epistemological level. People in the Third World are not interested in whether or not the Bible contains some metaphysical or revealed truth. The authority of the Bible can hide no longer behind an unchallenged belief that it is the Word of God, nor by an appeal to a church tradition that has been defined by white, male clerics. The poor, women, and other marginalized people are asking whether the Bible can be of help in the global struggle for liberation.

BIBLICAL INTERPRETATION AS DIALOGICAL IMAGINATION

To interpret the Bible for a world historically not shaped by the biblical vision, there is a need to conjure up a new image for the process of biblical interpretation. I have coined the expression "dialogical imagination," based on my observation of what Asian theologians are doing.

The Chinese characters commonly translated as dialogue mean talking with each other. Such talking implies mutuality, active listening, and openness to what one's partner has to say. Asian Christians are heirs to both the biblical story and to our own story as Asian people, and we are concerned to bring the two into dialogue with one another. Kosuke Koyama, a Japanese theologian, has tried to express this metaphorically in the title of his latest book, *Mount Fuji and Mount Sinai*. He affirms the need to do theology in the context of a dialogue between Mount Fuji and Mount Sinai, between Asian spirituality and biblical spirituality.[20] Likewise, biblical interpretation in Asia must create a two-way traffic between our own tradition and that of the Bible.

There is, however, another level of dialogue we are engaged in because of our multireligious cultural setting. Our fellow Asians who have other faiths must not be treated as missiological objects but as dialogical partners in an ongoing search for truth. This can only be done when each one of us takes seriously the Asian reality, the suffering and aspirations of the Asian people, so that we can share our religious insights to build a better society.

Biblical interpretation in Asia must involve a powerful act of imagination. Sharon Parks shows that the process of creative imagination involves the following stages: a consciousness of conflict (something not fitting), a pause, the finding of a new image, the repatterning of reality, and interpretation.[21] Asian Christians have recognized a dissonance between the kind of biblical interpretations we have inherited and the Asian reality we are facing. We have to find new images for our reality and to make new connections between the Bible and our lives.

The act of imagination involves a dialectical process. On the one hand, we have to imagine how the biblical tradition—formulated in another time and in another culture—can address our burning questions of today. On the other hand, based on our present circumstances, we have to reimagine what the biblical world was like, thus opening up new horizons hitherto hidden from us. Moreover, since the Bible was written from an androcentric perspective, we women have to imagine ourselves as if we were the audience of the biblical messages at those times. As Susan Brooks Thistlethwaite has suggested, we have to judge critically both the text and the experience underlying it.[22]

The term *dialogical imagination* describes the process of creative hermeneutics in Asia. It attempts to convey the complexities, the multidimensional linkages, and the different levels of meaning that underlie our present task of relating the Bible to Asia. This task is dialogical, for it involves ongoing conversation among different religious and cultural traditions. It is highly imaginative, for it looks at both the Bible and our Asian reality anew, challenging the historical-critical method, presumed by many to be objective and neutral. The German word for imagination, *Einbildungskraft*, means the power of shaping into one.[23] Dialogical imagination attempts to bridge the gaps of time and space, to create new horizons, and to connect the disparate elements of our lives into a meaningful whole.

To illustrate the meaning of dialogical imagination I shall discuss the ways in which Asian theologians have combined the insights of biblical themes with those found in Asian resources. We can discern two trends in the process today: the first is the use of Asian myths, legends, and stories in biblical reflection. The second is the use of the social biography of the people as a hermeneutical key to understand both our reality and the message of the Bible.

For some years now C. S. Song, a theologian from Taiwan, has urged his Asian colleagues to stretch their theological minds and to use Asian resources to understand the depths of Asian humanity and God's action in the world. He says: "Resources in Asia for doing theology are unlimited. What is limited is our theological imagination. Powerful is the voice crying out of the abyss of the Asian heart, but powerless is the power of our theological imaging."[24] To be able to touch the Hindu heart, the Buddhist heart, the Confucian heart, we have to strengthen the power of theological imaging.

C. S. Song demonstrates what this means in *The Tears of Lady Meng*,[25] which was based on a lecture he delivered at an assembly of the Christian Conference of Asia. Lady Meng was known for her courage in challenging the oppressive power of the king. Song takes this well-known legend from China, the story of Lady Meng, and weaves it together with the biblical themes of Jesus' death and resurrection. In another of his books, *Tell Us Our Names*, Song shows how fairy tales, folk stories, and legends—passed down from generation to generation among the common people—have the power to illuminate many biblical stories and other theological motifs. Song reminds us that Jesus was a master storyteller, who transformed common stories into parables about God's kingdom and human life.[26]

The use of Asian resources has stimulated many exciting and creative ways of rereading the scriptures. A theologian from Thailand, Maen Pongudom, interpreting the creation story in Genesis, argues that people of other faiths and traditions share certain essential ideas of creation found in the biblical story.[27] Archie Lee, a scholar of the Hebrew Scriptures in Hong Kong, uses the role of the remonstrator in Chinese tradition to interpret the parable of Nathan. In so doing, he seeks to relate the story of Nathan to the political context of Hong Kong. His creative rereading of the stories from two traditions shows that any "story has the unlimited power to capture our imagination and invite the readers to exert their own feeling and intention."[28]

Asian women theologians are discovering the liberating elements of the Asian traditions as powerful resources for reimaging the biblical story. Padma Gallup reinterprets the image of God in Genesis 1:27-28 in terms of the popular image of *Arthanareesvara* in the Hindu tradition, an androgynous image that expresses a half male and half female deity. She argues that "if the Godhead created humans in its image, then the Godhead must be a male/female, side-by-side, non-dualistic whole."[29] I myself have used Asian poems, a lullaby, and a letter of a female political prisoner to interpret the meaning of suffering and hope.[30] I have also used the story of the Vietnamese boat people in Southeast Asia to reappropriate the theme of the Diaspora.[31]

In her observations about the growing use of Asian resources in theologizing, Nantawan Boonprasat Lewis, a Thai theologian, makes the following perceptive remarks:

> The use of one's cultural and religious tradition indicates the respect and pride of one's heritage which is the root of one's being to be authentic enough to draw as a source for theologizing. On the other hand, it demonstrates a determination of hope for possibilities beyond one's faith tradition, possibilities which can overcome barriers of human expression, including language, vision, and imagination.[32]

The dialogical imagination operates, not only by incorporating the cultural and religious traditions of Asia, but also in the radical appropriation of our own history. We begin to view the history of our people with utmost seriousness in order to discern the signs of the time and of God's redeeming action in that history. We have tried to define historical reality in our own terms, and we find it filled with theological insights.

In Korean *minjung* theology, Korean history is reinterpreted from the *minjung* perspective. *Minjung* is made up of two Chinese characters that mean the common people, or the masses who are subjugated or ruled. *Minjung* is a very dynamic concept; it can refer to women who are politically dominated by men, or to an ethnic group ruled by another group, or to a race ruled by another powerful race.[33] The history of the *minjung* has often been neglected in traditional historical writing. They have often been treated as docile spectators in the rise and fall of kingdoms and dynasties. *Minjung* theology, however, reclaims the *minjung* as protagonists in the historical drama, for it is they who are the real subjects of history.

Korean theologians stress the need to understand the collective spirit—the consciousness and the aspirations of the *minjung*—through social biography. According to Kim Yong Bock, "The social biography is not merely social or cultural history: it is political in the sense that it is comprehensively related to the reality of power and to the 'polis,' namely the community. . . . Social biography functions to integrate and interrelate the dimensions and components of the people's social and cultural experiences, especially in terms of the dramatic scenario of the people as the historical protagonists."[34]

The social biography of the *minjung* has helped Korean Christians discover the meaning of the Bible in a new way. Cyris H. S. Moon reinterprets the Hebrew Scriptures through the social biography of Korea's *minjung*.[35] He demonstrates how their story—the constant threat of big surrounding nations and the loss of national identity under Japanese colonization—can help to amplify our understanding of the Hebrew Scriptures. On the other hand, he also shows how the social biography of the Hebrew people can illuminate the meaning of the Korean *minjung* story. Through powerful theological imagination Moon has brought the two social biographies into dialogue with one another.

The hermeneutical framework of the *minjung*'s social biography also helps us to see in a new way the relationship between Jesus and the *minjung*. According to Ahn Byung Mu, the *minjung* are the *ochlos* (crowd) rather than the *laos* (people). In Jesus' time they were the ones who gathered around Jesus—the so-called sinners and outcasts of society. They might not have been the direct followers of Jesus and were differentiated from the disciples. Furthermore, they were the people who were opposed to the rulers in Jerusalem.[36] Elucidating the relationship of Jesus to the *minjung*, theologian Suh Nam Dong says, in a radical voice, "The subject matter of *minjung* theology is not Jesus but the *minjung*. . . . Jesus is the means for understanding the *minjung* correctly, rather than the concept of '*minjung*' being the instrument for understanding Jesus."[37] For him, "Jesus was truly *a part of* the *minjung*, not just *for* the *minjung*. Therefore, Jesus was the personification of the *minjung* and their symbol."[38]

Social biography can also help characterize the hopes and aspirations of women, as Lee Sung Hee has demonstrated.[39] The question of whether Jesus can be taken as a symbol for the women of the *minjung* has yet to be fully clarified. Social biography is a promising hermeneutical tool because it reads history from the underside, and therefore invites us to read the Bible from the underside as well. Korean *minjung* theology represents one imaginative attempt to bring the social biography of *minjung* in Korea into dialogue with the *minjung* of Israel and the *minjung* in the world of Jesus. It shows how dialogical imagination operates in the attempt to reclaim the *minjung* as the center of both our Asian reality and the biblical drama.

LIBERATING THE BIBLE: MANY VOICES AND MANY TRUTHS

After this brief introduction to the history of the politics of truth in the Chinese Christian community and the dialogical imagination as a new image for biblical reflection, I would like to discuss briefly my own understanding of the Bible. I shall focus on three issues: 1) the sacrality of the text, 2) the issue of canon, and 3) the norm of interpretation.

The Sacrality of the Text

The authority of the Bible is based on the claim that it is Holy Scripture, that is, a written text of the Word of God. However, it must be recognized that this understanding of scripture (as divine revelation) is culturally conditioned; it is not found in other religious and cultural traditions, such as Hinduism and Confucianism. This may partly account for the relative fluidity of these traditions, which can often assimilate other visions and traditions. Nor do these traditions exhibit a crusading spirit seeking to convert the whole world.

Why has the Bible, seen as a sacred text, shaped western consciousness for so long? Jacques Derrida's deconstruction theory, particularly his criticism of the "transcendent presence" in the text and the logocentrism (primacy of the word as law) of western metaphysical tradition, offers important insights. In a volume of *Semeia* that focuses on "Derrida and Biblical Studies," editor Robert Detweiler summarizes Derrida's challenge to biblical scholarship:

The main characteristic of sacred texts has been their evocation and recollection of sacred presence—to the extent that the texts themselves, the very figures of writing, are said to be imbued with that divine immanence. But Derrida argues that such a notion of presence in writing is based on the false assumption of a prior and more unmediated presence in the spoken word; this spoken word in the religious context is taken to be none other than the utterance of deity, which utterance is then reduced to holy inscription in and as the text. For Derrida, however, written language is not derivative in this sense; it does not find its legitimacy as a sign of a "greater" presence, and the sacred text is not rendered sacred as an embodiment of an absolute presence but rather as the interplay of language signs to designate "sacred."[40]

The notion of the "presence" of God speaking through the text drives us to discover what that "one voice" is, and logocentrism leads us to posit some ultimate truth or absolute meaning that is the foundation of all other meanings. But once we recognize the Bible as one system of language to designate the "sacred," we may also be able to see the biblical text as one form of human construction to talk about God. Other systems of language, for example, that of Chinese characters, so different from the Indo-European languages, might have a radically different way of presenting the "sacred."[41] Moreover, once we liberate ourselves from viewing the biblical text as sacred in and of itself, we can feel free to test and reappropriate it in other contexts. We shall see more clearly how the meaning of the text is very closely related to its context, and we shall expect a multiplicity of interpretations of the Bible; as Jonathan Culler says, "Meaning is context-bound but context is boundless."[42]

The Issue of Canon

Canonization is the historical process that designates certain texts as sacred, and so authoritative or binding for the religious community. This process must be analyzed in the context of struggles for religious and political power. For example, scholars have pointed out that the formation of the canon of the Hebrew Scriptures took place within the power-play between prophets and priests. Moreover, the New Testament canon was formed in the struggle for "orthodoxy" against the so-called heretics, especially Marcion. Recent feminist scholarship has shown further how the biblical canon excluded elements of goddess worship that flourished in the Ancient Near East and how the New Testament canon was slowly taking shape in the process of the growing patriarchalization of the early church.

The formation of a religious canon is clearly a matter of power. As Robert Detweiler so aptly puts it: "A text becomes sacred when a segment of the community is able to establish it as such in order to gain control and set order over the whole community."[43] This was true both inside the religious group as well as outside of it. Inside the religious community, women, the marginalized, and the poor (in other words, the *minjung*) did not have the power to decide what would be the truth for them. Later, when Christianity was brought to other cultures, the biblical canon was considered closed, excluding all other cultural manifestations.

As a woman from a non-biblical culture, I have found the notion of canon doubly problematic. As my fellow Chinese theologians have long argued, Chinese Christians cannot easily accept a canon that denigrates their great cultural teachings and traditions. And as a woman, I acknowledge the validity of what Carol P. Christ has said: "Women's experiences have not shaped the spoken language of cultural myths and sacred stories."[44] Women need to tell our stories, which give meaning to our experiences. Christ continues, "We must seek, discover, and create the symbols, metaphors, and plots of our own experience."[45]

Indeed, I have begun to question whether the concept of canon is still useful. Claiming to safeguard truth, on the one hand, canon can also lead to the repression of truth, on the other. A closed canon excludes the many voices of the *minjung* and freezes our imagination. It is not surprising that feminist scholars of religion are involved in the rediscovery of alternate truths or the formulation of new ones. Rosemary Radford Ruether's book *Womanguides* is a selection of readings from both historical sources and modern formulations that are liberating for women.[46] Elisabeth Schüssler Fiorenza's reconstruction of the early Christian origins borrows insights from non-canonical sources.[47] Carol P. Christ describes women's spiritual experiences from women's stories and novels.[48] African American women scholars, such as Katie Geneva Cannon and Delores S. Williams, have emphasized black women's literature as resources for doing theology and ethics.[49] These stories of the liberation of women, as well as other stories drawn from different cultural contexts, must be regarded as being as "sacred" as the biblical stories. There is always the element of holiness in the people's struggle for humanhood and their stories are authenticated by their own lives and not the divine voice of God.

The Norm for Interpretation

Rejecting the sacrality of the text and the canon as a guarantee of truth, I also do not think that the Bible provides the norm for interpretation in itself. For a long time such "mystified" doctrines have taken away the power from women, the poor, and the powerless, for they help to sustain the notion that "divine presence" is located somewhere else and not in ourselves. Today we must claim back the power to look at the Bible with our own eyes and to stress that divine immanence is within us, not in something sealed off and handed down from almost two thousand years ago.

Because I do not believe that the Bible is to be taken as the norm by itself, I also reject the belief that we can find one critical principle in the Bible to provide an Archimedean point for interpreting the text as a whole. Rosemary Radford Ruether has argued that the "biblical critical principle is that of the prophetic-messianic tradition," which seems to her to "constitute the distinctive expression of biblical faith."[50] I think the richness of the Bible cannot be boiled down to one critical principle. The *minjung* need many voices, not one critical principle. Nor do I think that the prophetic principle of the Bible can be correlated with women's experiences generally, as Ruether suggests. Such a view assumes that the prophetic principle can be lifted from its original context and transplanted elsewhere quite apart from the cultural factors at work. Ruether fails to see that the method of correlation, as proposed by Tillich and Tracy, presupposes a Christian answer to all human situations, an assumption that needs to be critically challenged in the light of the Third World situation today.

Conversely, I support Elisabeth Schüssler Fiorenza's suggestion that a feminist interpretation of the Bible must "sort through particular biblical texts and test out in a process of critical analysis and evaluation how much their content and function perpetuates and legitimates patriarchal structures, not only in their original historical contexts but also in our contemporary situation."[51] The critical principle lies not in the Bible itself, but in the community of women and men who read the Bible and, through their dialogical imagination, appropriate it for their own liberation.

The communities of *minjung* differ from one another. There is no one norm for interpretation that can be applied cross-culturally. Different communities raise critical questions about the Bible, and they will find diverse segments of it addressing their specific situations. Our dialogical imagination has infinite potential to generate more truths, revealing hidden corners we have failed to see. While each community of *minjung* must work out its own critical norm of interpretation, it is important that we hold ourselves accountable to one another. Our truth-claims must be tested in public discourse, in constant dialogue with other communities. Good news for Christians might spell bad news for Buddhists or Confucians.

The Bible offers us insights for our survival. Historically, it has not been used solely as a tool for oppression, because the *minjung* themselves have appropriated it for their liberation. It presents many stories: of the slaves' struggle for justice in Egypt; the fight for survival of refugees in Babylon; and the continual struggle of anxious prophets, sinners, prostitutes, and tax-collectors. Today, many women's communities and Christian base communities in the Third World are claiming the power of this heritage for their own liberation. These groups, which used to be peripheral in the Christian Church, are revitalizing the Church at its center. It is the commitment of such people that justifies sharing and hearing the biblical story in our mutual search for a collective new religious imagination.

In the end we must liberate ourselves from a hierarchical model of truth, which posits one truth above many. This biased belief leads to the coercion of others into sameness, oneness, and homogeneity, excluding multiplicity and plurality. Instead, I suggest a dialogical model for truth: each has a part to share and to contribute to the whole. In the so-called non-Christian world, we tell our sisters and brothers the biblical story that gives us inspiration for hope and liberation. But it must be told with the open invitation: What treasures have you to share?

2

THE BIBLE, THE CRITIC, AND THE THEOLOGIAN

Asia is a multiracial and multicultural continent, the birthplace of many of the historical religions of humankind. Divided into seven major linguistic zones, Asia has numerous religious scriptures from the major religions that have shaped her cultures for millennia. In the past, the Christian notion of scripture has been defined by the Bible, but the time has come for theologians to look at the Bible within the larger multiscriptural context of Asia. A cross-cultural perspective enables us to understand the mode of transmission and reception of scripture as well as the potential and actual function of scripture "in the life of the imagination, its role as an organizer of ideas, images, and emotions, as an activating symbol."[1]

Interpreting the Bible in the context of Asia, Asian critics must clarify our own understanding of *Asia* and the interpretive space from which we speak. Our understanding of Asia must take into consideration the changing history and culture of the people. On the one hand, we cannot simply look back nostalgically to the past, as if Asia is always ancient, traditional, and unchanging. On the other hand, we must reclaim and reaffirm the national identity and cultural autonomy of the Asian people, so that we see ourselves through our own eyes. If the critic is not only an Asian, but a woman as well, she must also explain her understanding of women's experiences and female identity and her positioning within the wider feminist theological discourse.

In the long hermeneutical tradition of Asia, the study of scripture has never been a disinterested and uninvolved enterprise. The study of the wisdom of the past is meant for the use of the present. Reinterpretation of the Bible has played a key role in the formulation of liberation theologies, including black theology, Latin American theology, Asian theology, and theologies from women's perspectives. More recent biblical scholarship has increasingly demonstrated that androcentrism, classism, and racism are found not only in the history of interpretation but in the biblical text itself. The relationship between critical biblical studies and liberation theologies needs to be rethought in a more careful manner. This chapter discusses the complex relationship among the Bible, the critic, and the theologian in the Asian context.

THE BIBLE IN RELIGIOUSLY PLURALISTIC ASIA

The diverse religious traditions in Asia have different modes of transmission. Some Asian traditions have ancient scriptures that date back several thousand years, while others do not. Some emphasize the oral transmission of scripture; others put the accent on learning the written text. In the West the term *scripture* has often been used synonymously with *Bible*, but Wilfred Cantwell Smith observes that there is a shift of meaning of *scripture* from specific to generic, "from the Western word 'scripture's designating the Bible to its being predicated of a broad series of texts around the world."[2] During the past decade, scholars have delved much deeper into the diversity of the world's scriptures and their relationships with different communities. A significant number of books have been published in the comparative study of scripture.[3]

Many complex and technical questions arise in discussing scripture as a cross-cultural phenomenon. *Scripture*, understood as a generic term to denote "any sacred or religious writing or book," may not always be applied to the Chinese *jing* (originally the warp of a textile) or the Buddhist *sutra* (words spoken by the Buddha). William A. Graham identifies four clusters of issues when he discusses the problems of using scripture as a conceptual category: 1) the radical diversity in form and content of the notable scriptures in the world's religions, 2) the fact that some texts, such as the Chinese classics, are considered peripherally "religious," yet they have scriptural qualities, commanding reverence and functioning as normative in faith and morals, 3) the difficulty of delimiting scripture in terms of primary and secondary texts, as in the case of the voluminous Buddhist writings, and 4) the different media of expression, both in written and oral forms.[4]

While Graham is helpful in clarifying an understanding of scripture on the theoretical level, I am more interested in how the different notions of scripture play out in the actual life of Asians. I would like to use my own encounter with different scriptures in Hong Kong as an illustration. My parents, like most Chinese people in Hong Kong, practice Chinese folk religion; scripture never has been important in their religious life. In high school I was taught selections from the Confucian classics, which were included in the study of Chinese language and literature. Nobody objected to teaching Confucian classics in the schools, since they are seldom viewed as religious scriptures. In addition to the Confucian classics, Buddhist schools teach their students Buddhist *sutras*, and Christian schools, the Bible.

Since I did not go to a Christian school, I encountered the Bible in a school fellowship for Christians and in the Anglican church, which I attended from my teenage years. My school fellowship group was very evangelical, espousing a literal interpretation of the Bible; in contrast, the Anglican church emphasized a balance of Bible, reason, and tradition. I was thus exposed to a pluralistic understanding of the Bible from the very beginning. Occasionally

I had the opportunity to listen to Buddhist monks chanting their scriptures when I visited the temples or to hear Daoist scriptures chanted in traditional Chinese funerals. It was not until college and graduate school that I was taught some Buddhist and Daoist texts in a more academic way.

My experience of the multiscriptural Chinese context suggests that scripture is a very fluid and dynamic concept. First, many scholars in the history of religions have pointed to the relational character of scripture.[5] A text becomes scripture because of the way people receive it and enter into relationship with it. Its status changes over time, depending on the social and political circumstances and the transformation of its receptive community. Confucian classics are a case in point. The Confucian classics assumed unprecedented high status in the second century B.C.E. when Confucianism was made the official tradition of the state. Throughout the centuries, Chinese literati studied the classics both for self-cultivation and in preparation for the civic examination to become government officials. Rodney L. Taylor has argued that the Confucian classics assumed scriptural quality in terms of the reverence they commanded and the influence they exerted among such scholars.[6] But with the abolition of the examination system in the early twentieth century and the repeated humiliation of China by foreign powers, the Confucian tradition was radically challenged and its classics were criticized as conservative and backward-looking. Its authority was further downplayed in the anti-Confucius campaign during the Cultural Revolution (1966-1976). Students in China during that time were not taught to read Confucian classics at all. In Hong Kong, Confucian texts are studied as part of Chinese literature and civilization; they do not assume scriptural quality as in earlier times.

Second, in a multiscriptural context, one is exposed to different kinds of scripture at the same time. While each kind of scripture may claim authority over its adherents, the fact that different scriptures coexist makes relative the claim of ultimate authority for any one of them. The Chinese have been conscious that there are diverse teachings, and one can find meaning and guidance in more than one of them. In fact, the meeting of different traditions and creative appropriation among them have given birth to exciting new ideas and sometimes even new traditions. The encounter of Buddhism with the Chinese tradition resulted in a new religious movement, Zen Buddhism. The infiltration of Confucian thoughts into Buddhist and Daoist thinking resulted in the flowering of Neo-Confucianism in the eleventh and twelfth centuries.

Last, it is important to point out that in a multiscriptural world, the boundaries that delimit scripture are not that rigid. The scriptures are available not just to one community but to diverse groups. From everyday experience one knows that scriptures function differently even within the same religious community. Buddhist scholars who study the *Lotus Sutra* at the university treat it more like a literary classic, while adherents of folk Buddhism often revere the text for having sacred or even magical qualities. Although the concept of canon existed in some traditions, for example, in Buddhism and Daoism, the canons are so huge that few have access to all of them.[7] While scholars and religious authorities might be interested in canon as a regulating concept, it does not figure prominently in folk culture. Even today, very few individuals can afford to own a set of Dao Zang (Daoist Collectanea), bound in sixty volumes in the Taiwanese edition. In many Asian societies, religious organizations are not as highly institutionalized as the Christian Church in the West. In the Confucian tradition no functional equivalent to the priesthood exists, nor are there tangible religious institutions for standardizing and transmitting precepts.[8] Few Asian religions have a centralized agency to uphold the unity of truth and the authority of the canon. Numerous sects make competing claims as to what books are authoritative.

Given the pluralistic and diverse understanding of scripture in the Asian context, the idea of truth neatly contained within the covers of one single book, as in the case of earlier European Christian understanding of the Bible, is foreign to most Confucians, Hindus, Buddhists, and Daoists. It is unfortunate that a narrow and exclusive view of the Bible flourished during the century of mission and so became the dominant position held by many Asian churches. The emergence of a fundamentalist understanding of the Bible coincided with the period of rapid expansion of colonialism. Fundamentalism, as James Barr has pointed out, has a root in the revival movements on both sides of the Atlantic, originating in a time dominated by doctrinal exclusiveness, when the distinction between "true" and "nominal" Christian faith was central.[9] Such an intolerant brand of Christianity fell into a strained relationship with the more inclusive and multiscriptural ethos of Asia, alienating many Asian people.

Since the Bible exists as one of many scriptures, it is important to develop a multifaith hermeneutics in Asia. As R. S. Sugirtharajah of Sri Lanka has pointed out, this includes sensitivity to scriptural texts of other faith communities and the sustenance they provide for their adherents. Moreover, biblical interpretation should not simply aim at a Christian audience, because prospective readers are likely to include Buddhist friends or Hindu colleagues. The task for a biblical interpreter, Sugirtharajah says, "is not only to discover how to live as a member of a multifaith society, but also how to interpret the scriptural texts taking note of the presence and the spiritual intuitions of people of other faiths."[10]

Facing the twenty-first century, Christians need to learn that the Bible is not meant simply for Christians but also for the global community. Just as Confucian scholars are breaking through the Sinocentric study of Confucianism, Christian scholars must open up their religious resources for the use of all humankind. The question shifts from how the Bible can be normative for the Christian community to how it can bear meaning for the survival of human beings and the planet. Our goal is not to generalize and distill abstract principles from the Bible in order to apply them prescriptively in other situations, but rather to respect the particularity of the stories, derived often from a Jewish context, and to learn from them religious insights for dealing with the common issues that face all human societies. The role of the interpreter is not to use the Bible to guard a narrow and self-centered understanding of Christian identity but rather to destabilize all imperialistic claims of truth for the liberation of all.

ON BEING AN ASIAN WOMAN CRITIC

Asia is a diverse continent, eluding simple caricature and easy definition. Meeting at Seoul, Korea, a group of Asian theologians wrote:

> Asia . . .
> We pause in silence
> Before the awesome reality of Asia,
> Her vastness, variety and complexity,
> Her peoples, languages, cultures.
> The richness of her history
> And the present poverty of peoples.[11]

Asia is not just a geographical area but a social and cultural construct, signifying different things according to the social location of the person. For Aloysius Pieris of Sri Lanka, what makes Asia distinct from other areas is her poverty coupled with religiosity.[12] Aruna Gnanadason of India, having grown up amid enchanting temples, shrines, and religious sites, pays special attention to the spirituality of Asians.[13] C. S. Song's Asia is made up of myths, legends, and folklore, which provide endless resources for constructing story theology.[14] Living in a country constantly under threat from surrounding powerful nations, Chung Hyun Kyung of South Korea remembers the *minjung* of Asia and the plight of women.[15] Having grown up in the British colony of Hong Kong, where people's participation in political life has been limited, I am always concerned with the historical destiny and cultural identity of the Asian people.

Asia is always multiple, fluid, and changing. To say one is Asian does not imply an essence of "Asianness," or an abstract Asian subjectivity, or a generalized Asian womanhood. When Asian theologians call themselves Asian, the term signifies the consciousness of belonging to the history of particular groups of people; inheriting the myths, languages, and cuisines of certain cultures; commitment to looking at the world and ourselves from particular vantage points; and solidarity with the struggles and destiny of specific peoples. For these theologians the term *Asian* has an identifiable set of meanings: shared colonial history, multiple religious traditions, rich and diverse cultures, immense suffering and poverty, a long history of patriarchal control, and present political struggles.

From another vantage point the meaning of Asia can be seen in relation to the West, since Asia and the West are closely linked not only in terms of colonial history but also in terms of cultural imagination. Whether named the

Orient or the East, Asia is conceived to be the Other in the western mind. The projection of meanings onto the term *Asia* in different periods of western history reflects much about how the West understands itself. Because of a long colonial history, Asians have often been forced to see ourselves in the constructions of the West and our history as an extension of western history. The postcolonial quest for national and cultural identities involves the dual process of constantly deconstructing the western view and reconstructing Asian identity. The meaning of *Asian* is unsettling not only because of Asia's own complexity but also because of her shifting relation with the West.

The term *women* has likewise become highly problematic in feminist discourse. The most heated debate in current feminist theory centers around the essentialist versus the social constructionist understanding of gender. It has been pointed out that feminists in the 1960s and 1970s often assumed that women share an essential womanhood, without paying sufficient attention to class and race issues. Such an essentialist position faces a two-pronged criticism. On the one hand, women of color criticize the racist and ethnocentric assumptions of white feminists; on the other hand, there is the postmodern critique of totalizing discourse and the construction of the transcendental human subject.[16] In the past decade the accent in feminist theory has been on the politics of identity and the differences among women. Some theorists have begun to ask whether the terms *women* and *women's experience* can be used without falling into meaningless generalizations and abstractions.

Yet several important theological texts written by women of color in the 1990s do not shy away from using the experiences of specific groups of women as a hermeneutical tool of analysis. Chung Hyun Kyung's *Struggle to Be the Sun Again* says Asian women's theology is "very Asian," and "very women."[17] Delores S. Williams's *Sisters in the Wilderness* uses Hagar's story both to elucidate black women's experiences and to evaluate the classical theological tradition.[18] Ada María Isasi-Díaz's *En la Lucha* employs the ethnographical method to gather data about Hispanic women's religious experiences.[19] These writers do not share an essentialist understanding of "women," because they have constructed Asian, black, and Hispanic women's identity in terms of difference, rather than of essence. They are also conscious of the fact that Asian, black, and Hispanic women, as groups, are very diverse. They use specific women's experience rather as a discursive strategy, as Sharon D. Welch has pointed out, for challenging the canons, methods, and doctrines of Christian theology and white, middle-class constructions of female identity.[20]

As an Asian, I have found essentialist versus anti-essentialist debate of white women to be culturally specific, that is, deeply rooted in Greek metaphysics, in the universalizing colonial discourse during the age of imperialism, and in the current western controversy on language and its representation.[21] In contrast, Chung, Williams, and Isasi-Díaz understand women's identity more in the context of political engagement, of defining the struggle of particular groups of women, of relating to a specific history, and of accountability to a certain people. The adjectives *Asian, black,* and *Hispanic* do not connote a certain essence but a political *positioning* in the feminist discourse and struggle. Elaborating the meaning of positioning, Linda Alcoff says: "If we combine the concept of identity politics with a conception of the subject as positionality, we can conceive of the subject as nonessentialized and emergent from a historical experience and yet retain our political ability to take gender as an important point of departure."[22]

Thus to call myself an Asian woman signifies the self-awareness that sees the construct of gender from a particular culture as a vantage point from which to look at the world and to act politically. This understanding of Asian woman is multilayered, fluid, and open to new and continual reinterpretation, depending on shifting contexts and changing historical circumstances. It does not refer to a particular set of attributes or characteristics. It does refer to one position relative to the network of relations in our world. It signifies at once the complexity of Asia, the unsettling relationship with the West, the diversity of women's experiences, and the different positioning within the feminist discourse. The perspective of Asian women is partial, situated, and context-bound, without any false claims to be universal, objective, or value-neutral.[23]

As an Asian woman critic, I am painfully aware that contemporary mental and intellectual space is controlled by the cultural hegemony of the West, the white gaze, and the unceasing self-representation of the male. In the field of biblical studies the domination of western epistemology, presuppositions, methods, and solutions is particularly acute. Just a few decades ago the historical-critical method was the reigning paradigm and the only acceptable academic method for studying the Bible. Today there are other competing paradigms, such as literary criticism, rhetorical criticism, sociological criticism, ideological criticism, and reader-response criticism. While these methods do open new doors to the Bible, most of them nevertheless develop from the same cultural matrix and from the western anxiety about truth, knowledge, and language.

The emerging field of feminist interpretation of the Bible is dominated by European and American scholars. Many of their works build on white male scholarship (even if they refute and argue against it) and white feminist theory. Their scholarship emerges within the western women's movement, which is defined by the interests of white middle-class women, as well as within the movement of women-church, which has yet to foster stronger links to Third World women and minority women in Europe and America. Thus, when they recover the suppressed voice or hidden history of the women in the Bible, many have not paid sufficient attention to the fact that women in biblical times were divided by race, class, religion, and culture, just as women are today. Influenced by their social and cultural background, their feminist reading is also colored by their construction of female identity, which should not be taken as representative of all women.

When we look at the Asian scene, there has not been enough substantial discussion on indigenous approaches to Asian biblical hermeneutics.[24] Some attempts have been made to interpret the Bible from the context of religious pluralism and from the perspective of the poor and marginalized.[25] More vigorous debate and scholarly exchange on Asian hermeneutical methods and principles need to take place in the future. While some Asian male theologians and biblical scholars have paid attention to the oppression of Asian women, they have not dealt self-consciously with the issues of androcentrism in the biblical text and with the extent to which their male privileges have colored their interpretation.

An Asian woman critic is, therefore, an Other to western biblical scholarship, to white feminist theological discourse, and to male-dominated theological scholarship in Asia. Such multiple marginalities create a multiple consciousness that shuns dualistic or binary thinking and rejects a "simple and reductive paradigm of 'otherness.'"[26] With multiple subjectivity an Asian woman critic sees not only the fusion of horizons but also the rupture of the order of things, not only the cogency of argument but also the arbitrariness of the construction of meanings, not only unity and coherence but also dissymmetry and fragmentation. The possibilities of creative dialogues because of the multiple consciousness of the female investigating subject enable multiple readings and open new arrays of interpretation.

To articulate an indigenous Asian biblical hermeneutics, an Asian woman critic must honor and respect reflections on the Bible by Asian women and not become preoccupied only with other critics' theories. As I was reading Asian women's biblical reflections published in various anthologies and in *In God's Image*, my initial response was that they are *unacademic*, meant more for a pastoral context than for the theological academy. R. S. Sugirtharajah is right in observing that a growing gap exists between the logical, sophisticated, and internally coherent western biblical scholarship and Asian readings of the Bible that rely on intuition, imagination, and the free association of ideas.[27] Then I began to see that I was using the norms and standards of western biblical criticism to judge these writings. I did not ask about the cultural and religious matrix that made it possible for their intuition and imagination to occur. Neither did I ask whether these women's writings might reflect another logic, one that is not abstract, deductive, and one-dimensional. It was not until I had done some research on the transmission of religious scripture in Asia that I began to see that some Asian Christian women used an oral form of interpretation that is pervasive in Asian religious life. These women have their hermeneutics; I could not hear or understand it, because I did not have the adequate tools to do so.

This discovery leads me to pay attention not only to how Asian scriptures are transmitted but also how they are interpreted. Asia is unique in the Third World in that it has produced a very long hermeneutical tradition on religious scriptures quite independently of the West. From a cross-cultural perspective it is valuable to compare the nature and task of hermeneutics in the East and in the West. Several interesting questions arise: What is the relationship among hermeneutics, language, and reality in different cultural contexts? How does a changing historical consciousness influence the way we look at ancient

writings, including scripture? How do different hermeneutical traditions attempt to lift up or silence the voices of women?

In addition to deepening our knowledge of Asian heritage, we have to
broaden our horizons beyond the western intellectual landscape. Third World
theologians together with Asian American, African American, Hispanic, and
Latino theologians have made substantial contributions to the theological disciplines. People who were once colonized, subjugated, and oppressed have
built up a provocative counter-discourse in opposition to the hegemony of the
West. For example, Barbara Christian and Henry Louis Gates have contributed to literary criticism based on African American literature.[28] Ashis Nandy
of India helps us understand the psychology of colonialism, both in respect to
the colonizers and to the colonized.[29] Edward W. Said has discussed the constitution of subject in the British and French colonial discourse, and Gayatri
Chakravorty Spivak has placed postmodernism and poststructuralism in an
international frame.[30] Similar to these scholars, an Asian critic inhabits many
worlds and sometimes finds herself situated between worlds. Creative scholarship can come about by bringing these different worlds together.

THE USE OF THE BIBLE IN THEOLOGY

During the 1960s and 1970s the Bible served as a foundational source for
liberation theologies in the Third World and black theology in the United
States. For Latin American theologians the Bible clearly reveals that God has
a preferential option for the poor and that Christ is the liberator of humankind. James Cone describes black theology as biblical theology. The norm of
black theology, for him, must take into consideration the liberation of black
people and the revelation of Jesus Christ.[31] Likewise, South African theologians, such as Allan Boesak and Desmond Tutu, have stressed the importance
of the Bible as the Word of God and the God of the Bible as the God of
liberation.[32]

A similar neo-orthodox approach to the Bible can be seen also in the earlier work of Asian theologians. C. S. Song, for example, argues that Asians
need not waste their energy taking numerous theological detours through
western Christian norms and culture in order to understand the Bible. He suggests that the Bible can be transposed directly from Israel into their own Asian
situation.[33] Kosuke Koyama, too, is concerned to contextualize the Bible in
the culture and history of Asia. He contrasts the "crucified" mind as revealed
in Jesus Christ with the "crusading" mind seen in many Christians. His Bible
studies bring into focus the striking contrasts that exist between biblical images and images in contemporary society.[34]

These theologians view the Bible as a primarily liberating source. For them,
the problem lies in the fact that it has most often been interpreted by white,
western men or given a distorted reading by colonial oppressors. Once its
liberating potential is recovered through a subversive reading, the Bible can

be a powerful tool for conscientization of the people and a weapon against the oppressors. However, such uncritical acceptance of the Bible is no longer tenable in the 1990s because of the growing awareness of Third World and black theologians that there are both liberating and non-liberating strands in the Bible, and there is no non-ideological identification or appropriation of the Bible.

Using the story of the Egyptian slave woman Hagar as her heuristic key, Delores S. Williams charges that

> when non-Jewish people (like many African-American women who now claim themselves to be economically enslaved) read the entire Hebrew testament from the point of view of the non-Jewish slave, there is no clear indication that God is against their perpetual enslavement.[35]

Nor do the writings in the New Testament clearly oppose the institution of slavery. Poignantly she asks: "One wonders how biblically derived messages of liberation can be taken seriously by today's masses of poor, homeless African Americans, female and male, who consider themselves to be experiencing a form of slavery—economic enslavement for the capitalistic American economy."[36]

From another context, South African theologian Itumeleng J. Mosala criticizes the theological identification of the Bible as the Word of God. He writes:

> The insistence on the Bible as the Word of God must be seen for what it is: an ideological maneuver whereby ruling-class interests evident in the Bible are converted into a faith that transcends social, political, racial, sexual, and economic divisions. In this way the Bible becomes an ahistorical, interclassist document.[37]

Mosala understands the Bible to be "the product, the record, the site, and the weapon of class, cultural, gender, and racial struggles."[38] The task of a black hermeneutics of liberation is to recover the origin and history of these struggles within the text and to engage them in today's ongoing human struggles.[39]

Furthermore, many women theologians in the Third World have spoken out against the Bible's androcentric bias. Aruna Gnandason, for one, notes:

> The Bible cannot be spontaneously reappropriated by women, i.e., we cannot just read the Bible through the eyes of women, because we cannot deny the fact that the Bible *is* an androcentric text written by men in a patriarchal context.[40]

Moreover, several Asian women theologians radically challenge the limitation of using just the Bible and Christian sources for theology. As Chung Hyun Kyung has pointed out, many poor Asian women approach a variety of religious sources for religious sustenance and empowerment. She challenges

Asian theologians to move away from doctrinal purity and risk "survival-liberation centered syncretism."[41]

The Bible will continue to be a source for Christian theology in Asia, given its importance in the life of the church, especially in the Protestant tradition. But how can a book that has been used to oppress Asians, one that is itself a product of gender, class, race, and cultural struggles, be used in today's faith communities? There are no easy answers to this difficult question. I suggest the following steps to approach it.

First, Asian theologians must demythologize the sacred authority that is associated with the Bible. To demythologize is to "render contingent and provisional what is widely considered to be necessary and permanent."[42] We must begin to challenge the claim of biblical authority from the perspective of Asian women, from our painful colonial history, and from a pluralistic understanding of scripture in our cultures. In colonial discourse the Bible was viewed as the "civilizing agent," since "colonialism minus a civilizational mission is no colonialism at all."[43] Asian Christians must debunk western claims that the Bible is the sole revelation of God because such claims reinforce the ethnocentrism and cultural hegemony of the West. They contribute as well to the perception among Asians that the Bible is the book of foreign aggressors. Instead of fencing ourselves in with a closed and rigid understanding of Christian identity, Asian Christians should learn from the wisdom garnered by our ancestors through the millennia that truth is available in many diverse forms and teachings.

Second, Asian theologians must demystify the ways the Bible has been used to reinforce unequal relationships between the East and the West, women and men, and the rich and the poor. To demystify is "to lay bare the complex ways in which meaning is produced and mobilized for the maintenance of relations of domination."[44] This demystifying process is especially complex and multilayered for Asian women theologians. It involves challenging the biblical interpretations introduced by the missionary brand of Christianity and unmasking the power dynamics that lie behind the so-called neutral and objective biblical scholarship in the western academy. Furthermore, it has to evaluate in a critical way the counter-discourses that are being introduced by both Asian male theologians and Euro-American feminists, learning from their strengths and pointing out their limitations.

Third, Asian theologians need to construct new models of interpreting the Bible based on the culture and history of Asia and the struggles of Asian peoples. Such construction needs to take into consideration the history of biblical interpretation in different Asian contexts, the use of the Bible in Asian theologies, and the tension created by the western-oriented academic study of the Bible in some parts of Asia and the fundamentalist heritage of many Asian churches. In constructing these new models Asian theologians must be conscious of the ways our own interpretations are colored by gender privilege, class background, and professional or social status. On a continent where for millions of people survival itself is precarious, it is an enormous privilege to have been educated and to have the luxury to participate in intellectual discourse. For me, the critical test for any theological construction is how much it contributes to lessening human suffering; to building communities that resist oppression within the church, academy, and the society; and to furthering the liberation of those among us who are most disadvantaged, primarily the women and the children.

3

Toward a Dialogical Model
of Interpretation

In the past two decades some Asian theologians have paid attention to the interaction of the Bible with the cultures, religions, and histories of the Asian peoples. We have begun to investigate numerous aspects of scriptures; these include the relationship between the text and the interpretive community; diverging understandings of scripture; different assumptions of the task of hermeneutics; and the encounter among different religious scriptures in specific Asian contexts.[1] Some scholars have attended to the social, psychological, and cultural roles of scripture in shaping the religious life of a people.

As we search for new models for biblical interpretation in Asia, it is important that we tap into Asia's rich cultural heritages. Coming from a Chinese background, I have found that the discussions on the nature of the Chinese language, the Chinese mode of thinking, and the transmission of Chinese culture provide invaluable insights into the nature of hermeneutics. Building on such rich resources I articulate more carefully the theoretical basis for a dialogical model of biblical interpretation (to which I allude in Chapter 1).

Different models of biblical interpretation have divergent and sometimes contrasting images, or metaphors, for the Bible. For example, the Bible is revered as the *Word of God* in the doctrinal interpretation of the church. In the past two centuries the Bible has often been studied as a source of ancient *history* in seminaries, divinity schools, and religion departments of the western academy. Contemporary literary criticism treats the Bible as *literature* to be analyzed with the help of formalism, structuralism, poststructuralism, and other current literary theories.[2] My own proposal of a dialogical model of interpretation imagines the Bible as a *talking book*, engendering conversations and creating a polyphonic theological discourse. Instead of treating the Bible as a dead document, Christian communities have continuously used the language of the Bible to speak about their own experiences and to construct meanings to meet the needs of the local situation and the challenge of the time.

LANGUAGE, THOUGHT, AND KNOWLEDGE

The linguistic turn in contemporary intellectual debates focuses on the representation of reality in language, the connection between language and the thought process, and the relationship among language, subjectivity, and social relations. As a Chinese woman whose mother tongue is Cantonese, a dialect of the southern part of China, I enter this discussion from a linguistic background fundamentally different from people who speak Indo-European languages. The Chinese language, written as characters instead of using an alphabet, has functioned as "a sort of European hallucination," as Derrida says.[3] On the one hand, Leibniz suggested that the Chinese script could be the basis of a universal script.[4] On the other hand, some western scholars have labeled the Chinese language primitive, defective, unscientific, and incapable of expressing abstract thought.[5] Such observations display ethnocentrism because the linguistic features of Indo-European languages were invariably taken as the criteria to judge all other languages. Understood in its own social and cultural context, the Chinese language can illustrate an alternative set of assumptions and attitudes about language, offering illuminating insights for cross-cultural comparison.

While other ancient civilizations in the Middle East and in Egypt gradually adopted an alphabetical system, Chinese is the oldest civilization that has continued to use characters as a system of writing. The earliest form of Chinese writing has been found on shells and oracle bones dating from the second millennium B.C.E. Unlike some other cultures, the Chinese did not attribute sacred value to their written language.[6] Classical Chinese is a written language with its vocabulary and grammar, but it is not tied to any one system of pronunciation. Thus a passage in classical Chinese may be read in the pronunciation of any dialect of the speaker. The same word sounds very different when read in Mandarin, Shanghainese, or Cantonese,[7] since these dialects vary among themselves as much as French from Spanish or German from Dutch.

Since the founding of the People's Republic of China in 1949, there has been a movement to use one language for all China. Chosen as the common language (*Putonghua*), Mandarin, the dialect of Beijing, has become the medium for all public communication; it is taught in all Chinese schools. Nevertheless, various dialects are still widely used in the southern part of China. The Cantonese-speaking people of South China and Hong Kong are especially proud of their language. They have even created non-traditional characters for their colloquial words and expressions.[8] Modern Chinese dialects can be classified into seven major groups: Mandarin, Wu, Gan, Xiang, Hakka, Yue (Cantonese), and Min. In a country of over one billion people, the diversity of dialects allows for ethnic and regional differences.

In the Chinese language "there is no close, detailed correspondence between the written and the spoken word."[9] The relation between the sound of the word and the written symbol is largely arbitrary. This means that there is no "one voice" that can be traced from the written to the spoken word, and Derrida's concept of "logocentrism" cannot be applied easily to the Chinese case. The actual sound of Old Chinese is still much in the realm of specula-tion.[10] Whereas the written language has provided a basis of unity for the Chinese for two thousand years, people speaking different dialects must claim the language as their own by appropriating it into their phonemic system, tones, and accents. Soviet thinker M. M. Bakhtin's observation of the hetero-geneous nature of language is highly relevant here: "The word in language is half someone else's. It becomes 'one's own' only when the speaker populates it with his own intention, his own accent, when he appropriates the word, adapting it to his own semantic and expressive intention."[11]

As a writing system the Chinese language has both advantages and disad-vantages. The graphic quality of the Chinese characters gives aesthetic value, and calligraphy is a form of highly appreciated art. To master the Chinese language, one has to learn to write, pronounce, and remember the meaning of several thousand characters. Thus the transmission of the Chinese cultural heritage has relied on the literati, a group of people who could afford to de-vote time for protracted learning. Even though learning is valued in China, the spread of literacy is hindered by such a writing system. Further, Chinese women in traditional China were not given the same opportunity for educa-tion as men. Except for some women in the southern part of Hunan, who have developed a written language for women,[12] the majority of Chinese women relied on oral tradition to pass along their wisdom from generation to genera-tion.

Unlike the Indo-European languages, Chinese is not inflected to indicate case, number, person, tense, and so forth. A Chinese word can be used as a noun, verb, or adjective. Chinese grammar is, therefore, very different from that of inflected languages. With no word morphology, the meaning of each Chinese word depends on its context—the function of the word in the whole discourse. Furthermore, classical Chinese has no punctuation, and its sen-tence structure does not follow the subject-predicate format found in western languages. A sentence in classical Chinese can freely omit the subject; it can consist of a predicate or a verb phrase.

Although I do not subscribe to the idea of language determinism, I think the way our language is structured does influence our mode of thinking. As Chinese philosopher Zhang Dongsun has pointed out, Chinese logic is very different from Aristotelian logic because of the difference in language struc-ture. The traditional type of subject-predicate proposition is absent in Chinese logic.[13] According to Zhang, western logic is very closely related to the verb "to be" in western languages: "Because the verb 'to be' has the meaning of existence, the law of identity is inherent in Western logic."[14] In contrast to the "identity-logic" of the West, Chinese logic can be referred to as "correlative-logic." Chinese thought puts no "emphasis on exclusiveness, rather it emphasizes the relational quality between above and below, good and evil, something and nothing."[15]

Since Chinese characters lack inflection and classical Chinese texts are unpunctuated, it is important to conceptualize basic sentence units and delineate the boundaries of sentences. This is very difficult unless the sentences are short, simple, and in dialogue form. According to Chen Qiyun this may explain why many of the classical Chinese philosophical discourses are in dialogical form, introduced by "saying," "questioning," or the fictitious "some said." He cites the Shang Oracle Texts and the *Analects* as examples.[16]

This contrasting approach to language implies a different understanding of the purpose of knowledge. While Greek thinkers emphasized metaphysics and logic, Confucius' understanding of knowledge took a different route, as Benjamin I. Schwartz has noted:

> To Confucius knowledge does begin with the empirical cumulative knowledge of masses of particulars (particulars which may, however, include such items as the meaning of a poem) and then includes the ability to link these particulars first to one's own experiences and ultimately with the underlying "unity" that binds this thought together.[17]

Since the phenomenal world is always in flux and changing, Plato posited a world of ideas that is eternal and unchanging. Unlike Plato, Confucius made no such claims. He did not suggest we move "from the chaos of the world of particulars to a realm of eternal forms," because, for him, the *dao* remains "indissolubly linked to the empirical world," as Schwartz suggests.[18]

Classical Chinese thinkers spent very little time speculating about abstract propositional truth or constructing theories of metaphysics. Chad Hansen radically questions whether the Chinese have a concept of truth as understood in the western sense.[19] In general, the Chinese philosophers were more interested in moral philosophy and in the social and pragmatic function of language. Charles Peirce's distinction among three ways of theorizing about language is helpful for our discussion here. When we talk about language, we can relate it to the world (semantics), relate it to itself (syntax), and relate it to its social context (pragmatics). "Semantics uses terminology such as 'meaning,' 'concept,' and 'designation' as well as 'truth.' Syntax typically includes talk of word classes, rules, and characterizations of sentencehood. Pragmatics focuses on speech as an activity, on the emotive force of words, and on the roles of social conventions."[20] Chinese philosophy focuses more on pragmatics— on the correct use of language to provide guidance for action, to shape social relations, and to transmit a moral vision of society.

Like Plato and other Greek philosophers, Confucius was quite concerned with the relation of language to reality, but he approached the question from a different viewpoint. Western philosophers display a deep anxiety and mistrust about language. They have been concerned about the validity of language in its representation of reality, the truth-claim of a proposition, and the relation between the language sign and its referent. In contrast, Confucius and other Chinese philosophers did not see the problem as a crisis of language but rather of the human abuse and distortion of language. The misuse of language, for Confucius, arises not so much out of intellectual failure, as Socrates would have assumed, but out of selfish and ulterior motives.[21]

In Chinese thought there is no separation of the transcendent and the immanent, the human and the natural, the historical and the cosmological. This is much related to the correlative-logic and non-exclusive classification in Chinese culture. Learning is not seen as grasping intellectually a body of metaphysical or abstract eternal truth. In the Confucian tradition, learning is for the cultivation of the individual person and the ordering of human society. According to Du Weiming, the Confucian tradition understands the self to be a center of relationships, not an isolated entity. Self-cultivation, in the Confucian sense, is the process of "the broadening of the self to embody an ever-expanding circle of human relatedness."[22] With these assumptions of language, thought, and theories of knowledge, the Chinese understand the nature of hermeneutics not as seeking after absolute truth, but as searching for wisdom for practical living. Such an orientation allows more room for dialogue, for difference, and for multiplicity.

A DIALOGICAL MODEL OF INTERPRETATION

Drawing on resources from my own culture and Asian theologians' discussion of the Bible, I would like to further clarify the assumptions of a dialogical model of interpretation of the Bible. A dialogical model takes into consideration not only the written text but also oral discussion of the text in different social dialects. It invites more dialogical partners by shifting the emphasis from one scripture (the Bible) to many scriptures, from responding to one religious narrative to many possible narratives. It shifts from a single-axis framework of analysis to multiaxial interpretation, taking into serious consideration the issues of race, class, gender, culture, and history. It emphasizes the democratizing of the interpretative process, calling attention to the construction of meanings by marginalized people, to the opening up of interpretive space for other voices, and to the creation of a more inclusive and just community.

Our discussion of the Chinese language suggests that even with a language that attaches so much importance to the written form, we cannot overlook how people speaking different dialects appropriate the language as their own. Contemporary study of the Bible has focused too much on the written text without paying sufficient attention to how the Bible is related to the faith community and how people actually appropriate biblical language in their lives. Since oral transmission of scripture is prevalent in Asian religious life, a preoccupation with the written text cannot help us understand the lively process by which the Bible is told and retold by Asian Christian men and women.

In the Asian churches the relation between the written and oral dimension of the Bible is very complicated because few Asian Christians know the original languages of the Bible—Hebrew and Greek. We read different translations of the original text and talk about it using thousands of Asian dialects. I find Bakhtin's discussion of dialogism and heteroglossia helpful to conceptualize such a pluralistic use of the Bible in Asia. Bakhtin emphasizes that each social group speaks its own social dialect, according to class, religion, generation, region, and profession:

> The internal stratification of any single national language into social dialects, characteristic group behavior, professional jargons, generic languages, languages of generations and age groups, tendentious languages, languages of the authorities, of various circles and of passing fashions, languages that serve the specific sociopolitical purposes of the day, even of the hour . . .[23]

In the Asian context we may need to extend Bakhtin's categories to include race, ethnic group, and gender as well. These different social dialects may be "juxtaposed to one another, mutually supplement one another, contradict one another and be interrelated dialogically."[24] Dialogism describes the constant mixing of the intentions of both speakers and listeners, the need of inflection of past utterances to say something of one's own, and the way that any form of speech must position itself stylistically among other existing forms.[25]

Building on Bakhtin's work, Evelyn Brooks Higginbotham has suggested we use the dialogic model to characterize the Christian church:

> I characterize the church as a dialogic model rather than dialectical, recognizing "dynamic tension" in a multiplicity of protean and concurrent meanings and intentions more so than in a series of discrete polarities. Multiple discourses—sometimes conflicting, sometimes unifying—are articulated between men and women, and within each of these two groups as well.[26]

This allows us to see the church not as a monolithic edifice, but as a community where multiple discourses occur. Applying this model to the interpretation of the Bible, we will not focus simply on the author's voice or on the "orthodox" interpretation of the church leaders; instead, we will investigate the ways different groups of people in the Christian community create meanings out of the Bible from their different social backgrounds. We will also examine how these different interpretations create a multiplicity of meanings that interact with and condition one another. Women, too, do not speak with one voice.[27] A dialogical model highlights the possibilities of different readings according to our race, class, culture, and sexual orientation. What is exciting in the current discussion of the Bible is that people who used to exist at the margins of church and society are beginning to be heard. Their radical biblical interpretation often challenges the established methods of biblical criticism.

A dialogical model of interpretation emphasizes that Christian churches exist in dialogue with other human communities, including different faith communities. In multireligious Asia, we do not have one scripture, but many scriptures, not one religious narrative, but multiple religious narratives. In the past, Christians in Asia were encouraged to see our world and ourselves narrowly through one grand narrative: the Bible. This is very limiting because it rules out many possibilities and requires that all alternative narratives be subsumed and suppressed into it. Moreover, Christians are charged to *tell* the biblical narrative to others, but not to *listen* to other religious narratives in a reciprocal manner.

In contrast, a dialogical model suggests the genuine possibility of responding to many different narratives at the same time, of trying out different versions of each story, and of creating alternative narratives. Sometimes we recognize ourselves in stories from our own tradition; at other times we see ourselves more vividly in other peoples' myths and stories.[28] Those of us who have multiple identities often cannot tell who we are except by combining many different narratives. This requires us to imagine ourselves situated in various narratives in a dynamic way, with roles that are changing and shifting. Jean-François Lyotard suggests that we imagine ourselves as narrator, listener-reader, or actor within the different narratives. The listener of one narrative can become narrator of another, the narrator of one becomes the reader of another, the actor of one, the narrator of another. Thus, we can allow the different narratives to intersect and interact in new ways, opening up possibilities for alternative narratives or even counter-narratives.[29]

A dialogical model understands the self not as an isolated, monolithic identity but as a center of multiple relationships. It eschews the idea of an autonomous and transcendent subject doing the thinking and interpreting. Instead, it imagines the act of interpretation as a multilevel discourse that goes on within ourselves and with others. In this view consciousness comprises an inner dialogue, which is influenced by the social environment through the language we have acquired. People who have multiple identities have multiple subject positions when they converse with themselves and others. For example, I can assume the position of an Asian theologian when talking to western Christians. On another occasion, I can be a Christian talking to a Buddhist, a Muslim, or a Sikh in interreligious dialogue. Furthermore, I can assume the subject position of a woman offering critiques of both the Asian traditions and Christianity.

Women who experience multiple oppression insist that the politics of identity must be analyzed with regard to race, class, gender, sexual orientation, and culture.[30] African American feminist theorists emphasize the multiplicative effect of racism, classism, sexism, and heterosexism, as well as the need to examine their intersection with historical and cultural specificity.[31]

Higginbotham, for example, points to race as a metalanguage in her analysis of the racialization of gender and class in the United States.[32] In Asian societies, where sex tourism has become so institutionalized, we have to examine the sexualization of gender, race, and class in global terms. And as Audre Lorde points out, we need to deal not only with "the external manifestations of racism and sexism" but also "with the results of those distortions internalized within our consciousness of ourselves and one another."[33]

Biblical interpretation cannot follow a single-axis framework, whether it is race, class, or gender. In *Biblical Hermeneutics and Black Theology in South Africa*, Itumeleng J. Mosala argues that black theologians should break ideologically with bourgeois hermeneutical assumptions and contribute to the struggle of the black working class. Using a historical-materialist method of analysis, he pays relatively little attention to the issue of gender, an oversight he tries to correct in his more recent writing.[34] Aloysius Pieris's *An Asian Theology of Liberation* addresses the questions of *many poor* and *many religions* in Asia. In the book's preface the author laments his failure to integrate feminist concerns in his analysis of oppression in the Third World.[35] This omission affects his interpretation of the Bible. For example, in his discussion of the poor in the Bible, he fails to see that the poor consist of both men and women and that their oppression may be different.[36] On the other hand, using historical, literary, rhetorical, poststructuralist methods, or a combination of different approaches, many Euro-American feminist biblical studies treat gender oppression as a binary system of male over female, and they discuss "women" without integrating class and race into their analysis.

A dialogical model must adopt a multiaxial framework of analysis. We cannot talk about the class composition of the society of Israel or of the early Christian community without talking about race and gender. We cannot talk about women in the Bible without realizing that the women are of different classes and races. We cannot talk about race relations between Jews and Gentiles without attending to class and gender as well. An integrative method must take into consideration gender, race, class, and cultural differences all at once.

My proposal of a dialogical model emphasizes plurality of meanings, multiplicity of narratives, and a multiaxial framework of analysis. While some of these emphases may sound like postmodernism, they are rooted in the religious pluralism of Asia, the diversity of Asian dialects, the experience of multiple Otherness, and the thought patterns shaped by the Chinese language and East Asian culture. Plurality and multiplicity were an integral part of Asian culture, language, and religion long before the rise of postmodernism in the West.[37] We have to avoid superimposing a European framework on the development of Asian hermeneutics, which must remain rooted in its own specific cultural context.[38]

Following the Chinese theory of language, I underscore the pragmatic dimension of language and the social and political implications of interpretation. A dialogical model emphasizes that a text is not a free-floating object in its own right, because the processes of creation, transmission, and interpretation of a text are embedded in the social, cultural, and political matrix of society.[39] The meaning of a text cannot be found by tracing it back to the voice of God or of its author, nor can it be limited to the "original meaning" of its *Sitz im Leben*. Multiple meanings are created in public discussion, creative dialogue, and sometimes heated controversy. I agree with Elisabeth Schüssler Fiorenza that truth is not a metaphysical given but a "multiple, polyvalent assembly of voices."[40] A dialogical model welcomes new voices and new dialogical partners to further democratize the interpretive process. Enlargement of the interpretative space is possible only with the opening of social space and the creation of a more inclusive community, such that the Other can find its own voice without being suppressed and absorbed into unanimity.

THE BIBLE AS A TALKING BOOK

Different models of interpretation have offered a variety of specific images or metaphors for the Bible. The doctrinal model understands the Bible to be the Word of God. Those who favor this model include many who believe in verbal inspiration and those who use the Bible as proof-text to support their own theological positions.[41] This model is concerned with the Bible as God's revelation and the certainty of faith. The authority of the Bible is based on the assumption that the "voice" of God speaks through the text. In Bakhtin's terms, this model only allows for monologue because it demands obedience of the audience and precludes any other response. Furthermore, it superimposes its own context onto others, because it does not take into consideration historical and cultural specificity in the construction of meaning.

The historical-critical method treats the Bible as history. This model provides more room for dialogue because it differentiates between God's voice and the voices of those who wrote the Bible. It sees the Bible as an ancient document, emerging out of specific communities during particular historical periods. However, this method as practiced in the academy is interested more in a dialogue with the past than in a dialogue in the present. Through vigorous historical research, scholars who favor this model seek to determine what the Bible meant, without the concomitant interest in what the Bible means today. In other words, this model takes more seriously diachronic dialogue rather than synchronic dialogue.

Several new images of the Bible have been suggested by feminist biblical scholars and theologians.[42] Elisabeth Schüssler Fiorenza regards the Bible as a historical prototype, that is, as a formative root-model, rather than as a mythical archetype with timeless universal truth: "To read the Bible not as an unchanging archetype but as a structuring prototype is to understand it as an open-ended paradigm that sets experience in motion and makes transformation possible."[43] The strength of this approach is that it recognizes fully the historical context of biblical text without trying to apply it prescriptively to other contexts. It faces squarely the fact that the experiences generated by the root-model can be both liberating and oppressive to women, especially because of the unequal gender relations inscribed in the text. Furthermore, it shifts the focus away from issues of authority and canon to the feminist subject of interpretation, the practice of liberationist reading, and the collective transformation of tradition.

Schüssler Fiorenza's notion of the Bible as a historical prototype is rooted in her rhetorical model for a historical reconstruction of the lives of women in early Christianity. On the one hand, she challenges the historicist position, which tries to go behind the text to uncover in a "scientific" way "truth" about the past. On the other hand, she separates herself from the apolitical postmodern position, which argues that there is no reality outside the text.[44] While her position is forged in the midst of intellectual debate about postmodern and feminist theories, women of other cultural contexts may not face similar challenges. For example, many Asian peoples have commonly looked to their classics, or scriptures, more for religious and moral insights than for any historical truth. Recent studies on the hermeneutics of African American women indicate also that black women have always been more interested in relating the Bible to their life experiences than in the historical context of biblical texts.[45]

As a root-model, the Bible tells us very little about the lives of non-Jewish women, poor women, and slaves. Feminist New Testament scholars provide us with information about the women of property who were traveling missionaries with Paul, patrons of the apostles, and leaders of house churches, but not much information about poor and slave women. Until we know more about how poor women and slave women actually participated in the "discipleship of equals,"[46] we cannot simply rely on the Bible as our historical prototype without caution.

Instead of looking at the Bible from a historical point of view, theologian Sallie McFague suggests we look at the Bible as a poetic classic.[47] As a classic, the Bible has enduring centrality for all those who call themselves Christians. McFague emphasizes the Bible's intrinsic authority, alluding to its ability to speak with power to many people across the ages. She agrees with David Tracy that in the classics "we recognize nothing less than the disclosure of a reality we cannot but name truth."[48] On the other hand, she maintains that the Bible is poetic, underscoring the fact that it is rich, diverse, and open to many interpretations. Qualifying *classic* with *poetic*, McFague points to the "reforming and revolutionary power" of the Bible.[49] McFague's approach has the advantage of criticizing an idolatrous use of the Bible while addressing the Bible's seeming irrelevance in the modern world. McFague argues that as a model, the Bible should not be identified in an idolatrous way as the literal Word of God, and as a poetic classic, it continues to speak universally as do other great poetic works.[50]

Several questions arise regarding the value of McFague's image of the Bible in an Asian context. McFague does not explain whether the Bible differs from other western classics, such as the writings of Homer and Virgil.[51] As noted above, the differences and similarities between *classic* and *scripture* are an issue when we use the concept of scripture cross-culturally. McFague's acceptance of the intrinsic authority of the Bible and its universality for different peoples across the ages does not take into consideration the way the Bible has been used in the colonial discourse. When calling the Bible a great poetic work and a classic, both McFague and Tracy operate more from a hermeneutics of consent than a hermeneutics of suspicion. They have not dealt adequately with the harsh reality that the Bible also discloses: a hierarchical social order in which slavery and male domination are seldom challenged. While the Bible is certainly an enduring classic and a great cultural code of western civilization, Asian Christians have yet to find a hermeneutical method to overcome the alienation they feel as they try to relate the biblical world, colonial Christianity, and their own reality.[52]

I would like to offer another image of the Bible based on a dialogical understanding of biblical interpretation. The Bible can be seen as a "talking book," inviting dialogue and conversation.[53] The image of a "talking book" is taken from Henry Louis Gates in his discussion of the tradition of African American literature. The juxtaposition of *talking* with *book* signifies the fascinating relationship between the written and the oral in African American culture. Severed from their homeland and culture in Africa, black people were forced to learn the master's language in order to express themselves and to communicate with one another. Yet black people have constantly changed the signifying practices of the master's language and used the master's tongue in a double-voiced way.[54] A clear example is in their use of the Bible to express their experiences under slavery and to construct an African American tradition. As Cheryl Townsend Gilkes notes: "Fragments of the Bible found in songs, sermons, and prayers represent important evidence of this cultural imagination."[55] The image of talking book points to the subversive reading and imaginative use of the Bible by people who are subjugated and colonized. They have used a foreign book to talk about their own liberation; they have modified the master's tongue and used it to speak about justice and freedom.

There are several advantages to seeing the Bible as a talking book. First, it shifts the discussion away from an undue emphasis on the authority of the written text to the community of faith that is talking about the Bible and talking with one another. Second, it highlights the importance of the oral transmission of scripture in the religious life of Asia. Even in the West the primary mode for transmitting the contents of the Bible was oral until literacy became more common during the last two centuries. Third, as a talking book, its meaning is not fixed but open to negotiation in the discursive context. Fourth, it invites us to listen to the multiplicity of voices, filling in for the voiceless and uplifting the voices that have been marginalized. Fifth, it implies that truth is not sealed off or handed down from the past but is to be found in open discussion, honest conversation, and creative dialogue. History is not just to be recorded and studied but, more important, to be remembered and retold in order to guide us in the present.

Several issues must be clarified in my use of the metaphor of talking book. I do not assume the Bible to be a perfect talking book, speaking the language of freedom and justice without ambiguity. I fully agree with Renita J. Weems that the prevailing voices embedded in the Bible are male, elitist, patriarchal, and legitimated: "The voice of the oppressed in the end is not the predominant voice. In fact, theirs is a voice that could be viewed as random aberrant outbursts in a world otherwise rigidly held together by its patriarchal attitudes and androcentric perspective."[56] Given that the dominant voices in the Bible are those of privileged males, I am interested in knowing how women can hear these voices differently, using the biblical language not as an instrument of their own oppression but as a source for their empowerment.

We have to hold *talking* with *book* in order to appreciate the tension in the metaphor. Through the Bible we hear the song of Deborah, the oracles of Amos, the parables of Jesus, the plea of the hemorrhaging woman, and the testimony of Paul. We hear a plurality of voices speaking different social dialects from all sorts of backgrounds. We do not hear them directly, but through reported speech, which as Bakhtin says is "of speech within speech, utterance within utterance, and at the same time also speech about speech, utterance about utterance."[57] We have to understand the dynamic interrelationship between the speech being reported and the speech doing the reporting. This requires us to pay attention to the relation between oral transmission and the written document of the Bible, the framing of discourse by the author, the multilevels of the dialogue, and the possibilities of reframing the retelling in the present situation.

The Bible is neither the first nor last word. It is not the first word because its language necessarily borrows from and builds on the language of its time. It is not the last word because Christians all over the world continue to make the Bible "talk." As a talking book, it depends on the community of faith to bring it to life. Reading against the grain, many Third World theologians, feminist theologians, and minority scholars in the United States are transforming, interrupting, subverting, and recontextualizing biblical language. The circle of conversations needs continuously to be widened, and new people need to be brought in. It is hoped that the Bible will not elicit conversations only among Christians, but that people of other faiths, too, will find it a source for continuous dialogue.

4

HEARING AND TALKING

Oral Hermeneutics of Asian Women

In women's groups, at church meetings, and in the Y.W.C.A., Christian women in Asia study the Bible and discuss enthusiastically its implications for their lives. They dramatize biblical stories, retell gospel messages, and pose critical questions to the Bible from their own experiences. Bible study among Asian women is a communal event; they gather to talk about their own stories and the stories of the Bible, constructing new meanings and searching for wisdom for survival and empowerment. They treat the Bible as a living resource rather than as an ancient text closed in itself.

The importance of the aural/oral dimension in cultural and religious life has been emphasized by theologians and scholars in other cultural contexts. Teresa Okure of Nigeria has observed that the Africans were traditionally "a people of the word, not of the book."[1] Renita J. Weems points out that during slavery, black people in America were forbidden by law to learn to read and write. An aural hermeneutics emerged as the slaves evaluated the contents of the Bible through the critical lens of their harsh reality.[2] Likewise, Cornel West emphasizes the "kinetic orality" in black sermons, songs, prayers, and hymns. Its fluidity, rhetoric, and flexible oral stylizations of language, West maintains, "gave black church life a distinctively African-American stamp."[3] In Latin America, grassroots Bible study plays a crucial role in the life of the basic Christian communities, providing food for thought and sustenance for their ongoing struggle against injustice.[4]

In the past several decades interdisciplinary studies of oral and written traditions have yielded fruitful results, but such research has not been appropriated by the majority of biblical scholars. In *The Oral and the Written Gospel*, Werner H. Kelber suggests the main reason for this neglect lies in "the tendency among biblical scholars to think predominantly, or even exclusively, in literary, linear, and visual terms."[5] In order to study the strategies of oral hermeneutics by Asian women, we have to shift our attention from the written text to the women who are talking about the text. We need to emphasize that ordinary Christian women are interpreters of the Bible, and the insights they offer are no less important than biblical scholarship contributed by scholars in the academy. Furthermore, the study of oral hermeneutics requires us to learn from disciplines including linguistics, translation, anthropology, history of religions, and cross-cultural studies.

In this chapter I explore the strategies of oral hermeneutics by Asian women based on my own participation in women's Bible studies and relevant written resources. The first part presents a gender analysis of the transmission of scriptures in Asia, with special focus on the Bible, to provide a cultural and religious context to understand the oral hermeneutics of Asian women. The implication of orality and textuality for biblical interpretation will be examined in the second part. Finally, I shall analyze some examples of oral hermeneutics from Christian women in Asia.

TRANSMISSION OF SCRIPTURES IN ASIA—A GENDER ANALYSIS

On the diverse continent of Asia some of the religious traditions do not have scriptures; I shall limit the discussion here to those historical religions with a scriptural tradition. In the West *scripture* often means a written text— the Latin *scriptura* means "writing." The same is not true in Asia, where scripture can assume diverse forms. For example, the Vedas of the Hindu tradition have been transmitted orally from generation to generation, although writing was invented two and a half millennia ago in India. Scripture was considered more often to be spoken words rather than written texts.[6] Indian theologian Stanley J. Samartha has noted: "One has to go behind the written texts to the *sound* of the Word, recited and heard over long periods of time by the community, in order to see how words have functioned religiously in matters of faith."[7]

Comparable to the Bible, many Asian scriptures went through a period of oral transmission, some for a long period of time, before they assumed written form. The Confucian *Analects*, a compilation of the sayings of Confucius and his disciples, were recorded long after the death of the master.[8] The Daoist classic *Dao de jing* consists of sayings that embodied the spirit of a living tradition.[9] Shortly after the Buddha's death, his disciples met to recite his teachings in order to establish an authoritative body of doctrine for the future.[10] But the actual writing down of the Dharma was not achieved until hundreds of years later. The notable exception to this pattern of early oral transmission seems to be the Qur'an, which consisted from the outset as a written collection of Allah's revelations through his prophet Muhammad.

The question as to whether women participated in or played a role in the creation of Asian scriptures requires more study in the future. Tradition does not recount that women numbered among the seventy-two disciples of Confucius. In the case of Daoism, some of the basic motifs or concepts in *Dao de jing* date back to ancient times, when shamans—both male and female—played essential religious roles.[11] But the exact circumstances leading to the compilation of *Dao de jing* are still debated. In early Indian Buddhism women and men listened to the teaching of the Buddha and many women asked to be admitted to the monastic order.[12] It is not clear, however, whether they participated later in the writing and compilation of the sayings of the Buddha. In the Muslim tradition women did not participate in any meaningful way in recording and compiling the Qur'an, as far as we know.

Although the written text was revered in some Asian traditions, the dominant mode of scriptural transmission among the populace has been oral in most cases. Multiple relationships exist between scripture and its diverse receiving and interpretative communities, dependent on caste, class, and gender. The Hindus have developed elaborate techniques for verbatim memorization of the Vedas,[13] while the written texts are often regarded as the "defilements of the sacred sound."[14] The recitation of the Vedas was for centuries the responsibility of male priests of the brahmin caste to the exclusion of women and other castes.[15]

Islam is often referred to as a religion of the book, but in the everyday lives of the Muslim community, recitation of the Qur'an is far more wide-reaching and permeating than the study of the written text. In fact, the root meaning of Qur'an is "to recite" or "read aloud."[16] While Muslim scholars devote their energy to produce commentaries and studies of the book, common people recite and memorize oral texts. Until recently, Muslim women in general have not had equal opportunities to study the Qur'an. Attempts by women to challenge the teachings of the Qur'an have been suppressed, as in the recent death threat against the outspoken feminist writer Tasleema Nasreen of Bangladesh.

As for Confucianism, learning the classics has shaped the entire civilization of East Asia. Much of the learning has been done not simply through silent and private reading but through recitation, rote memorization, and conversation with teachers. While the masses learn portions of the classics, detailed exposition and exegesis of the words of the sages have been the responsibility of members of the literati. In China, girls who belonged to the upper class, or the families of literati, had opportunities to learn to read and study classical texts through private tutoring.[17] But until female education was made available in the nineteenth century, the number of women who could read and interpret classical texts was limited.

In the multifaceted tradition of Buddhism there are marked differences in the ways believers treat the sacred texts. On the one hand, the Buddhist scriptures are respected as authoritative, and for centuries scholars have been preoccupied with copying, translating, and interpreting the texts. In popular Buddhism scriptures sometimes assume a magical character, not unlike relics in the West. On the other hand, there is a deep-seated suspicion of texts, and words are seen by some as obstacles to direct religious experience, especially in the Zen tradition. Zen Buddhism emphasizes: "A special transmission outside the Scriptures; No dependence upon words and letters."[18] The recognition of the limits of human language and the embodiment of truth in ordinary things in everyday life is found also in Tibetan Buddhism. In some folk Buddhist traditions in China women have been religious leaders, custodians of secret scriptures from one generation to the next, and teachers of religious doctrines.[19] Buddhist nuns have opportunities to learn and study the *sutras* and helped to explicate them for the laypeople.[20]

The accent on oral traditions and transmission of sacred texts implies that the study of literary texts is not so important. Today, three-quarters of the world's illiterate population live in Asia, the majority of them women. Until female education becomes wide-spread and affordable, many Asian women, especially those in rural areas and poverty-stricken districts, will have access to sacred texts only through the aural/oral media: listening to religious texts recited at home, in the temples, and during religious ceremonies and festivals. Parts of the sacred texts are also told as myths, legends, epics, and performed as plays and festive dramas.

When the Bible was introduced into Asia, it encountered a cultural world with different understandings of sacred texts and diverse modes of transmission. During the century of mission the Protestant missionaries who arrived to preach the Gospel in many parts of Asia were influenced by the print mentality of the western world and invariably understood *scripture* to be a written text. Protestant missionaries, much more than their Roman Catholic predecessors, were engaged in translating the Bible into the languages of the people. Mission presses were set up and portions of the Bible, catechism, and religious tracts were widely distributed.

While Muslims regard Arabic as the revealed language, insisting that non-Arab believers learn to recite the Qur'an in its original language, Christianity assumes no single revealed language, and the Bible has been translated into different languages during the history of Christian expansion. As Lamin Sanneh has pointed out, the "success of Islam as a missionary religion is founded upon the perpetuation of the sacred Arabic."[21] In sharp contrast, the vitality of Christianity depends on the degree that its tradition is translatable into the local setting, and the radical pluralism and diversity of the biblical tradition.[22]

Because Asian languages usually include many different spoken dialects, missionaries decided to translate the Bible into the written languages and also the vernacular. The decision of the missionaries to render the Bible into the vernacular had significant repercussions. First, it elevated the status of the vernacular language. The printing press set up by William Carey in India produced religious materials in forty-four languages and dialects, and his linguistic research contributed to the renaissance of Bengali prose literature.[23] In China the Bible was translated into the literary style, Mandarin, regional dialects, and minority national languages.[24] Second, the use of the vernacular necessarily entailed borrowing the terminologies and concepts of the common people. In translating concepts such as heaven, hell, devil, soul, and repentance into Asian languages, missionaries had to borrow many of the terms from folk traditions. Third, the option for the vernacular also meant that the biblical text had to be recast in the spoken language and in the style that the common people would have told it orally.

Since most denominations required some knowledge of the Bible as a prerequisite for baptism, Christian missions were heavily involved in a literacy campaign. Sunday school for children, mission station courses, and catechism classes were offered to help prepare the candidates. For people who had not learned to read and write, the Bible looked mysterious and intimidating. For Asian women, who were excluded from any formal schooling, the process of learning to read the Bible could be both frustrating and liberating.

Much of the early missionary activity among women depended on the spoken word: for example, house-to-house visits, telling the gospel stories, singing hymns, and reciting the Lord's Prayer. Women were taught to read the Bible and a written catechism in Bible study classes, Sunday school, mission station classes, or catechism classes. Missionary work among women was initially led by women missionaries, but as mission work began to grow "Bible women" were employed to help teach women, especially in the rural areas. The involvement of Bible women and other lay women in the transmission of the Bible created women's fellowships, helping to nurture personal bonding among women within the patriarchal church and society.[25]

Christian missions were often the first to organize girls' schools in Asia to provide education for girls of the lower classes. Early girls' schools were meant to train future Bible women and the wives of pastors and evangelists. Both the Bible and religious instruction featured prominently in the curriculum. As time went by, the curriculum was expanded to include other subjects in the liberal arts, but the teaching of the Bible still occupied an important place. Among Christians the rate of female literacy was generally much higher than in the general populace. In some places Christian mission schools for girls served as catalysts moving local people to provide education for girls. The education of women remains one of the important legacies of the Christian mission in Asia.

The emphasis on female literacy and education reveals not only the gender dimension of the church's "civilizing" function, but a class dimension as well.[26] The Christian church and mission schools helped to nurture an emerging class of school teachers, female evangelists, Y.W.C.A. workers, medical doctors, and nurses. These women leaders, usually from urban areas, were instrumental in spreading new ideas of womanhood, which they learned from the Christian church and from their missionary teachers. But they have also been criticized for being westernized and identifying too much with the culture of the foreigners. Espousing middle-class values, these female leaders had a worldview very different from rural women and less educated women.

The tension between different classes of Christian women continues to exist today and manifests clearly in the ways they approach the Bible. Women who are more educated and who have received theological training tend to focus more on the written text. Some use western exegetical methods learned in seminaries to analyze the Bible. The majority of Asian Christian women, however, use free association and creative retelling of biblical stories to appropriate the Bible in their life situations. While academic study of the Bible can help clarify the androcentric language and worldview of the texts, oral hermeneutics of Asian women should not be ignored in our examination of feminist interpretation in Asia.

ORALITY AND TEXTUALITY IN BIBLICAL INTERPRETATION

The analysis of the Asian situation calls for closer attention to the implications of orality and textuality in the interpretation of the Bible. These implications are numerous: 1) the influence of the oral tradition on the written text, 2) the power dynamics behind the inclusion of some voices and suppression of others in the written account, 3) the relation between the oral and the written in the transmission process, 4) the influence of the medium of transmission on the various modes of biblical interpretation, and 5) the importance of understanding oral hermeneutics in feminist biblical interpretation. Trying to understand the implications of orality and textuality for biblical interpretation in Asia, I benefit from the insights of scholars who have studied the interaction between the oral and the written text of the Bible as well as from anthropologists, linguists, and cultural historians who have investigated the cognitive significance of orality.

In *The Oral and the Written Gospel*, Werner H. Kelber examines the complex process by means of which the oral kerygma was rendered into the written form. Contrary to Bultmann's presupposition that the written text was an automatic evolutionary progression from the spoken word, Kelber shows that the earliest canonical gospel, Mark, was actually a textual *interpretation* of the oral kerygma. Based on the growing research in the field of orality-literacy of many other disciplines, Kelber investigates the implications of the change of medium, the shift from a nonliterate to a literate and educated audience, and Mark's contribution to this process in producing the first unified narrative. Kelber reminds us that Jesus was an oral performer "moving from one place to another, surrounded by listeners and engaged in debate. . . . His message and his person are inextricably tied to the spoken word, not to texts."[27] But when these stories were written down, the concrete *event* that found expression in the oral exchange was lost, and the stories assumed a new medium, "in words that floated context-free, visually fixed on a surface, retrievable now by anyone anywhere, as the utterances of the oral kerygma had never been."[28]

But it is a mistake to think that once the gospels were written down, the oral stage was superseded, leaving few traces on the written accounts. In her study of the Gospel of Mark, Joanna Dewey notes that it lacks a tight plot structure, unlike the modern novel; instead, it has a more loose and additive plot development. This is because the gospel was composed with a listening audience in mind. Likening Mark to a piece of "interwoven tapestry," Dewey

emphasizes that "we need to pay more attention to oral hermeneutics in studying the Gospel."[29] Similarly, Charles H. Lohr has shown how oral techniques
influenced the actual composition of the Gospel of Matthew. Such techniques
include the use of formulaic language and repetitive devices for elaborating
unifying themes, the grouping of similar materials into individual sections,
the development of a leading idea through repetition of key words, and sym-
metry in structural arrangements.[30]

From a feminist point of view, the study of the relationship between oral
kerygma and written gospel expands our historical imagination of the roles
played by women in shaping the biblical tradition before it was fixed as texts.
We can easily imagine the women telling the stories of Jesus and how their
voices were largely suppressed in the written account. Dewey has argued that
although the gospels include stories about women, the actual voices of the
women who followed, listened to, and were healed by Jesus did not survive
in the writing process, because the gospels were written from an androcentric
perspective. Even when the stories do include women, Dewey observes, they
often present women in a skewed manner. For example, in the stories of the
anointing woman (Mark 14:3-9) and the widow's mite (Mark 12:41-44), the
women act but do not speak. Their actions became the subject of male discourse between Jesus and others.[31] In her study of the social make-up of the
Matthean community, Antoinette Wire maintains that the gender roles presented in the Gospel of Matthew reflect the assumptions of the community of
scribes who put the gospel in written form. At the same time, the inclusion of
stories about marginal individuals, especially those about women, seems to
her to suggest an underlying oral tradition in which "peoples' voices still
directly challenge others to faith."[32]

As the Bible assumed written form, the written text became primary. Oral
instruction was transformed into exegesis of this canonical body of literature.
Having traced the development of a primary oral culture, through a manuscript culture, to a print culture in the West, Walter J. Ong elucidates the impact
of this process on biblical interpretation.[33] It is noteworthy that before Johannes
Gutenberg introduced printing with movable metal type in Europe in 1447,
the circulation of costly Bibles in handwritten form was limited to the clergy,
theologians, monks, and the aristocracy. The social and historical location of
such persons influenced the interpretative process. The Bible was often used
as a proof-text for their own doctrinal positions, as a refuge for their ecclesi-
astical interests, and as divine sanction for their privileged positions within
the church and society. Ordinary people, who could neither read nor write,
were systematically excluded from participating in the creation of meaning
and knowledge that grew out of the study of the biblical text.

Since popular literacy in the West became a reality only during the last two
hundred years, for some eighteen centuries Christian common folk had access to the Bible primarily through the oral, aural, and visual media. Women's
knowledge of the Bible, whether in the East or in the West, came largely
through worship and preaching. In the liturgical setting of the church, the

Bible was never read in its entirety; instead, parts of the Bible were used to illustrate theological statement and principle.[34] Women were not encouraged to develop a comprehensive and critical understanding of the biblical message. Furthermore, their oral and aural hermeneutics of the Bible were dismissed as unimportant and were not subjected to careful study. To understand the divergent ways women have interpreted the Bible, feminist scholars cannot simply rely on the historical-critical method, literary criticism, and reader-response criticism, because these methods give primacy to the written text of the Bible.[35] Such methods fail to provide tools to analyze the negotiation of meaning in discursive contexts, the retelling of stories to meet the particular needs of an audience, or the thought processes that lie behind oral transmission. Moreover, many contributions of Third World Christians, especially women, who do not understand scripture rigidly as a "book," will be overlooked.

I have found the discussion of oral and literate cultures and the relationship between spoken and written languages that takes place today in the fields of anthropology, linguistics, and social and cultural history helpful for raising new questions about biblical interpretation. Instead of assuming the text to be fixed and given, these disciplines challenge us to problematize the nature and boundaries of a given text. Recent biblical scholarship distinguishes three different worlds to a specific text: the world *behind* the text, which may be uncovered through historical, archaeological and sociological methods; the world *of* the text, created by its use of language, narrative, and discourse; and the world *before* the text, constituted by the presuppositions and interpretative processes of its readers.[36] Such differentiation, though helpful, still assumes the primacy of the written text and reading as a largely silent act of the individual. It fails to take into consideration the performative function of sacred texts and the reconstruction of stories in a communal setting. As Ong has pointed out, in some oral cultures the stories are not memorized and repeated word for word each time. Instead, they are reconstructed and adapted to a particular context.[37] The text is considered to be dynamic and open-ended, not rigidly fixed by the written word.

The issue of orality and textuality has implications for the creation of meaning and the process of interpretation. Scholars who have studied oral and literate traditions point out that in an oral tradition, meaning is negotiated in the discourse, whereas in the literate tradition, meaning is often seen to exist in the written text. The former sees meaning as growing out of shared experience of the interaction between the communicator and the audience, while the latter focuses exclusively on the content of information or message. Understanding, in oral tradition, is more involved and subjective, achieved through a sense of identification with the speaker. In literate culture, it is more detached, logical, and analytical.[38]

Finally, there is the question of the thought process and assumptions about knowledge. Ong has observed that in oral tradition the thought process is more formulaic, elaborated, and "rhapsodic," whereas in literate tradition the thought process is analytical, linear, and sequential.[39] According to David R. Olson, truth in oral tradition lies more in common-sense reference to experience, while in literate tradition it resides in logical and coherent argument.[40] Jack Goody, an anthropologist who has studied oral and written cultures in West Africa, distinguishes between two different paths to knowledge. In oral culture the bulk of knowledge is passed on orally, in face-to-face contact among members of the family, clan, and village. In written culture knowledge comes from an outside, impersonal source (book) or is acquired in an extra-familial institution, such as a school.[41] He further observes that religious organization in oral cultures tends to be less rigid and more open, whereas religions that claim a written revelation tend to be more stratified and closed.

While there are differences between oral and literate traditions, these scholars are quick to point out that in many settings an interplay between the spoken and the written exists. The invention of writing did not end oral tradition, and the oral and literate coexist as a continuum. Furthermore, strategies learned from one medium can be used and applied to another. In the past, biblical interpretation has been largely an intertextual matter. I am arguing that an awareness of the different strategies in both oral and literate traditions will open new avenues for "listening" to the voices of Christians from the Third World, especially where the oral dimension is still paramount in people's lives.

EXAMPLES OF ORAL HERMENEUTICS BY ASIAN WOMEN

In this section, I will discuss strategies drawn from oral hermeneutics based primarily on my own experiences of Bible study with women in Asia and from other examples of biblical interpretation. My sources include Bible studies presented orally, conversations about biblical passages, and biblical reflections that show the use of oral style. These conversations and reflections are by literate women with a feminist consciousness. I recognize the need for future explorations of how women in oral cultures interpret the Bible. In citing these examples, I acknowledge the limits of written records in fully capturing the rhythm, tone, and emotional intensity of spoken language. On the other hand, these examples clearly show that an understanding of the oral tradition helps us to appreciate Asian women's interpretation of the Bible.

The first strategy is to give voice to women in the Bible. When Asian women gather to discuss and dramatize the stories of women in the Bible, they frequently imagine what the women would have said and acted in the situation. The reimagining of women as speaking subjects is important; as we have seen, the voices of women were often left out in the androcentric written account. There are several ways this silencing of women occurred, including 1) women's speech is left out, as in Mark's Gospel,[42] 2) women are admonished not to speak, as in the story of the Syrophoenician woman (Matt. 15:21-28), 3) women talk only to themselves; they are allowed private speech but not public speech. For example, the woman with a flow of blood speaks to herself: "If I touch even his garments, I shall be made well" (Mark 5:28), and 4) in extreme situations, women "voice" accusation of injustice done to them most powerfully through their abused or dead bodies, as in the cases of Hagar, Tamar, and Jephthah's daughter in the "texts of terror" studied by Phyllis Trible.[43]

Asian women theologians are well aware of the silencing of women in the Christian tradition. Lee Oo Chung, Sylvia Jenkin, and Mizuho Matsuda write in the introduction to *Reading the Bible as Asian Women*:

> During all these centuries, in the Biblical stories and texts, and in Christian documents, women's voices were silenced. With few exceptions, they are excluded from any opportunity to speak to the church. . . . Even the women in the Bible themselves gained no hearing, were misinterpreted or disregarded. But now, at the touch of Christ, by movement of his Holy Spirit in our time, the voices of women are crying out from the pages of Scripture.[44]

They encourage Asian Christian women to use creative ways to express their biblical reflections: through poems, pictures, dance, music, mime, storytelling, and testimonies. An example of recovering women's voice is a dramatization of the stories around Moses' birth in the book of Exodus by a group of Asian women. In Exodus 2, Moses' mother has no name and has no speech. In the dramatization by the Asian women she talks about the suffering of the Jewish people with other mothers, one of them Susannah:

Susannah: How our children suffer!
Jochebed: (Deep sigh) Yes. Their suffering breaks my heart more than anything. Our husbands work in the building site; we work in their homes as servants and yet our income is not enough for our livelihood.[45]

When Jochebed hears the decree to kill newborn baby boys, she laments:

Jochebed: It is a death sentence to my baby. The death sentence is on me and my family, on all Hebrew babies and families. God have mercy. Have mercy.[46]

Instead of giving up her son helplessly, as in the biblical account, the new version describes how Jochebed plans to save her baby with the cooperation of the midwives.

Another strategy drawn from oral hermeneutics is reframing the discourse and reconstructing the dialogue. An example is the revision of the conversation between the angel Gabriel and Mary (Luke 1:26-38) by Pearl Drego from India.[47] The story of the annunciation and Mary's response, in particular, has been subjected to various interpretations. Traditionally, Mary's reply has been taken to mean her submission and obedience to God. Feminist theologians have tried to reclaim Mary as a model of the new human being, a true disciple and an active participant in the drama of God's incarnation, who accepts her role through active consent.[48] But the discourse between Gabriel and Mary in the Lukan narrative is not framed on an equal basis. Gabriel does most of the talking and is clearly the more active partner in the conversation. Mary's words are few, and she is the one responding.

In her new version, Drego presents Mary as a full partner in the conversation, making her a full talking subject. Mary is portrayed as one who can read, draw, and play a musical instrument, and she is reading a book when Gabriel visits her. Drego reconstructs Mary's inner speech after Gabriel informs her that she will give birth to the Divine Child:

Mary: Somewhere deep within I knew I was being cared for in a special way and I cared for myself in a special way too. I am ready. It would have been nice to be just ordinary, to marry Joseph and have six or seven children. Yet, this choice has been stirring in my heart for some years. I've known it. I have seen you in dreams. I know that it will be much harder than I can tell. And yet if I don't say yes, the women of this earth will never be free, nor the men either. I can hear the women of the centuries, millions upon millions, their spirits call to me, "Maria, say yes, say yes, on behalf of all of us, you are doing it for all of us. God has chosen us and has chosen you from among us."[49]

Drego portrays Mary's response and transforms her act of submission to God into a positive response to the outcry of the women. When Gabriel warns that people will make up stories about how she was chosen for her compliance and obedience, Mary's reply is unequivocal:

Mary: Me, obedient? When I have defied so many of the laws and sayings of our Jewish patriarchs?[50]

In the course of the conversation Mary is invited to decide whether to give birth to a boy or a girl. After weighing the pros and cons, Mary gives her free consent to the birth of a boy. She rejoices that her virgin privacy will be protected and that God has bypassed rabbis and scribes to extend this invitation to her as a woman.

The retelling of stories and epics from the women's point of view is common in folk traditions in India. For example, women's songs may tell their own version of the Indian epic of Ramayana with characters and incidents not found in the written Sanskrit texts. While the text celebrates the birth of the hero, women's oral traditions in Telugu talk about the birth pangs of his mother and the suffering of his wife.[51] Using such oral technique in her culture, Drego reconstructs the episode of the annunciation. The reclamation of the voice of women in biblical narrative, the imaginative reconstruction of these women's encounters with God, and the presentation of these women as strong and defiant in respect to the patriarchal system play a significant role in the creative hermeneutics of Asian women,[52] and other oppressed women as well.[53]

The third strategy of oral hermeneutics is the blending of different narratives as if making a quilt or weaving a tapestry. I would like to use the Bible study I presented at the Asian Mission Conference organized by the Christian Conference of Asia in Indonesia in 1989 as an example. The Bible study, originally presented in dramatized form with movement, dance, and costumes, is reprinted as the Prologue of this book. I explain my background and women's way of doing Bible study, trying to establish rapport with the audience. The Bible study is not meant so much to convey information as to evoke a response. The oral performance tells simultaneously the story of the women in the ministry and passion of Jesus and the story of the courageous students who were massacred on the fatal night of June 4, 1989, at Tiananmen Square in China.

The Bible study tries to capture and express my double consciousness of my Chinese background and of the biblical tradition. It shows the "internal dialogization"[54] that weaves the two stories together. The contemporary story of Chinese students is not subordinated to the biblical story, nor is the Bible the text and the Chinese situation the context, as commonly understood in the process of contextualization in theology. On the other hand, the Chinese experience is not treated as the text, with the Bible and church tradition as the context for understanding, for there are many possible contexts. In oral performance the text is neither stable nor fixed. In retelling the story I have tried to *voice*, or speak, the Chinese *into existence* in an otherwise alien narrative.[55] Here, the meaning of both stories is negotiated and constructed precisely at the margin or boundary where one context pushes against another, alien context.

By framing the story in a new way, by playing with the borders, and by creating stylizing variants, this example shows that meaning is not fixed, but negotiated in the discourse. Oral representation retells the story in *one's own words*, transforming an external authoritative discourse into an internally persuasive discourse, as Bakhtin describes it.[56] For him, the latter's semantic structure is not fixed; its context is shifting, and its meaning is inexhaustible, inviting further dialogic interaction.

The last example is a Bible study I participated in at the Shanghai Y.W.C.A. A group of women theologians from Asia, Europe, and the United States visited churches and seminaries in China in the summer of 1990.[57] We had a Bible study on Genesis 2 with a group of Chinese Y.W.C.A. workers and local women leaders of the churches. Before the Bible study took place, we had spent a few days in China and learned about the changes in women's status after the revolution of 1949. The Chinese women leaders repeatedly told us that equality of women and men was guaranteed by the Constitution and the law, though women were still discriminated against in terms of jobs and educational opportunities.

In our discussion of the creation story in Genesis 2, the other Asian women theologians and I were conscious of the fact that the story was sometimes used against women because Eve was created second and she was to be Adam's helper (Gen. 2:18). But the Chinese Christian women in my group did not read the story in terms of male domination over female. One Chinese woman said that the term *helper* implied that Eve was a capable woman, that she could offer help to others. Living in a socialist country where equality between the sexes is emphasized in public discourse, these Chinese women focused on the complementarity of the two sexes in their interpretation. The experience has reminded me of the different social locations of women and the implications for our interpretation strategy. Coming from different cultures and societies, the women discussing the Genesis story have multiple subject positions and produce multiple interpretations. There is no single women's point of view and the meaning of the text is negotiated in the discursive practice.

These examples of strategies drawn from oral hermeneutics raise new questions about the text, context, and the process of interpretation. The Bible is understood to be a talking book, constantly eliciting further conversation and dialogue, instead of an external, privileged text handed down from a distant past. Building on the oral traditions indigenous in their culture, the oral hermeneutics of Asian women offer insights to women's creative appropriation of the Bible. Yet we have learned very little from such insights, because women's voices have not been taken seriously. I hope that biblical scholars and theologians can pay more attention to oral hermeneutics in the future, so that voices from the margins, including those of women, will not continue to be ignored.

5

SPEAKING MANY TONGUES

Issues in Multifaith Hermeneutics

At the seventh assembly of the World Council of Churches held in Canberra in 1991, a young woman theologian from Korea stunned the world by her electrifying keynote address. Accompanied by music, slides, dance, drums, and rituals, Chung Hyun Kyung addressed the assembly theme "Come, Holy Spirit—Renew the Whole Creation."[1] In the ensuing debate following her presentation, many issues were raised, including "inculturation, creation, inclusiveness, interreligious dialogue, syncretism, discernment of the limits of diversity, and pneumatology."[2] For many Asian theologians Chung has forcefully put the issue of Gospel and culture on the top of the ecumenical agenda.

The question of Gospel and culture is a perennial one in Asia. In the past, Asian theologians have attempted to bridge the gap between the Christian worldview and the Asian mindset through the process of indigenization. Indigenization means adapting Christianity to traditional Asian cultures so that it becomes rooted in the Asian soil. Christian faith was presented in Asian idioms, symbols, and concepts to make it less foreign. Motifs and doctrines in Christian teachings were compared to those in various traditions in Asia. Steeped in the Confucian tradition, Chinese Christians have sought parallels between the teachings of the Bible and those found in the Confucian classics.[3] In the Indian subcontinent various proposals have been made to place the cosmic Christ within the Hindu religious framework.[4]

Most of these earlier attempts were missiological in nature; that is, the aim was to show that Christianity was not a foreign religion, incompatible with indigenous cultures. Many believed that the essence of Christianity could be liberated from layers of western tradition in order to be represented in Asian styles. They did not question the basic doctrines of Christian faith or the teachings of the Bible.

Many contemporary Asian theologians have begun to question the validity and relevance of these earlier efforts. They no longer ask how *to present* the Gospel in Asian style, as if the Gospel were forever fixed and sealed off from the present. For them, the basic issue is *to discern* the Gospel anew in the living reality of contemporary Asia and in the day-to-day struggles of her peoples. Instead of adapting a colonial, western Christianity to Asia, they see the task of theology as reconceptualizing and reformulating the meaning of Christian faith. With a sense of pride and confidence in their own cultures, they do not assume the superiority of Christianity over other religions, and they are more daring in the use of Asian resources in doing theology.

Trying to relate Christianity to the religious traditions of Asia, some Asian biblical scholars and theologians have begun to articulate a multifaith hermeneutics. Multifaith hermeneutics assumes the willingness to look at one's own tradition from other perspectives, the maturity to discern both similarities and differences in various traditions, and the humility to learn from other partners in the conversation. Multifaith hermeneutics requires us to affirm that other religious traditions are as valid as Christianity. Since many Christians believe this view to be contrary to the Bible's seeming condemnation of other religions, I shall first discuss the relationship between the Bible and people of other faiths. Then, I shall give some examples of multifaith hermeneutics and analyze several issues involved in the interpretative process.

THE BIBLE AND PEOPLE OF OTHER FAITHS

Christian missionaries condemned the indigenous Asian religious traditions as idolatrous and full of superstition. This missionary heritage unfortunately still exerts great influence on Asian churches, which often have to struggle to survive in the midst of strong and vibrant Asian traditions. In the past, Asian Christians have too often set themselves *apart* from the people, instead of becoming *a part* of them. Today, Asian theologians have become aware that they are not separated from the religiosity of their people or from the common struggle for freedom and democracy in Asia. Recognizing the nourishment and strength other religions provide for their adherents, many have given up a crusading attitude and adopted the more pluralistic, open-ended approach of interfaith dialogue.

Interfaith dialogue acknowledges people of other faiths as fellow pilgrims. By promoting understanding and fostering mutuality and respect, the dialogical approach attempts to break down divisive barriers in an attempt to build wider human communities. Stanley J. Samartha, an influential figure who promotes interfaith dialogue in the ecumenical movement, writes:

When in multi-religious societies religious boundaries are sanctified and perpetuated by tradition, religions themselves become walls of separation rather than bridges of understanding between people. Therefore, the quest for communities today cuts across these boundaries, and persons of different faiths reach out to form communities of greater freedom and love. One of the ways in which Christians can be deeply involved in this struggle for community is through dialogue.[5]

The Bible presents problems for interfaith dialogue because it has often been interpreted as the Word of God, and much of the criticism leveled against dialogue is claimed to be based on the Bible. Opponents to interfaith dialogue can point to motifs and traditions in the Bible in support of their position. For example, the Bible claims there exists only one true God to the exclusion of all others. Having chosen the people of Israel among the nations, God enters into a covenantal relationship with them. Since all human beings have sinned against God, we can be redeemed only through the salvation brought about by Jesus Christ. The followers of Jesus were charged with the Great Commission to "make disciples of all nations" (Matt. 28:19).

Without overlooking such arguments, Wesley Ariarajah of Sri Lanka, former director of the sub-unit on Dialogue with People of Living Faiths of the World Council of Churches, offers several strategies to interpret the Bible that can be supportive of interfaith dialogue. First, he reminds us that the stories of the Bible are told from a particular perspective: "The other nations, their histories and faiths, are considered mainly from the standpoint of Israel."[6] The Bible reflects the self-understanding of the people of Israel, and other peoples may not share that understanding. Second, he lifts up an alternative tradition that emphasizes God's universal covenant with all nations and Christ's universal salvation for all people. God is the creator of all humankind and the Lord of all nations. The universality of Christ is not understood in exclusive terms, but as a basis for openness, sympathetic understanding, and dialogue with others.[7] Third, he cites examples of encounters between people of different faiths in the Bible. Jonah was asked to speak to the people of Nineveh, the capital of the Assyrian empire. Initially Jonah was reluctant, but eventually he went and called the people to repentance. The people of Nineveh responded to his message beyond all his expectations. In the vision of Peter recorded in the Acts of the Apostles, Peter was exhorted not to consider anything unclean that God has made clean (Acts 10:9-16). Defying the custom that Jews were not supposed to mix with Gentiles, Peter met with Cornelius, the Roman centurion, and this led to his conversion.[8] Fourth, Ariarajah argues that Christian witness is not contrary to dialogue. In fact, during the early stage of spreading the Gospel the apostles often adopted a dialogical approach. For example, Paul emphasized the death and resurrection of Jesus as the Messiah when speaking to his Jewish audience (Acts 17:2-4), but he opted for a more theocentric approach when talking to Athenians, who might not see the significance of Jesus in the Jewish worldview (Acts 17:22-23).[9]

Ariarajah emphasizes that religious pluralism is not only a concern of contemporary Asian Christians but was also a challenge to the Hebrew people and the early church. Indeed, Israelites lived among neighbors worshiping Baal, Asherah, Astarte, and other gods and goddesses. Similarly, the early church developed in the midst of numerous religious traditions. For many

Asian theologians the dynamic cultural exchange and religious interaction between the people of Israel and her cultural environment offer insights for Asian Christians living in today's pluralistic world.[10]

According to E. C. John of India, the Hebrew people adapted certain beliefs native to Canaan while rejecting others as unacceptable. As examples of assimilation he cites the identification of their God with the God El, the adaptation of the belief that the Temple was the dwelling place of God, and the idea of kingship. But the Israelites were also warned against sacrificing to Canaanite gods, feeling a false security based on the Temple and the Ark, and the dangers brought about by the institution of kingship. John suggests that the relationship between the faith of Israel and that of its neighbors was much more complex than we have assumed. He rejects earlier scholarship that emphasizes the uniqueness of the Hebrew Scriptures and points to the similarities and differences, the continuity and discontinuity between the religion of Israel and the cultural and religious traditions of the Ancient Near East.[11]

The adaptation of Israel to its cultural environment was not always a smooth process. The Hebrew prophets repeatedly warned against most forms of religious syncretism. Because the prophets' condemnation of other religions has created difficulty for Christians living in a pluralistic context, Asian theologians have begun to reevaluate the prophetic heritage. Some have interpreted the prophets in a positive light by placing them within their own religio-cultural times and political contexts. For example, George Koonthanam of India argues that the prophets were against the superficial sacrifices and the exploitation of the priestly class. For him, the prophetic teaching is relevant in the face of religious hypocrisy in Asia today when religious institutions care more for their own power than for the welfare of the people.[12]

While most Asian theologians tend to identify with the prophets, C. S. Song in a recent article urges his Asian colleagues to move beyond prophetic theology. Song says the prophets' emphasis on justice and their solidarity with the poor and the oppressed must be affirmed. But their vital weakness—the negative attitude toward other cultures—must not be overlooked. The prophets' failure to appreciate the "idols" as symbols with religious meanings and their exclusive attitude toward other religions have contributed to Christianity's hostility toward people of other faiths. Following the prophetic tradition, liberation theologians—both in Latin America and Asia—have emphasized the socio-political liberation of the people, while refusing to see the theological significance of the cultural and religious aspirations of the people. Song points out that when confronted with stories of oppression of the people, liberation theologians readily grasp the social and political implications of these stories, but they often fail to appreciate their religious and cultural implications for theology.[13]

Such varied interpretations of the prophetic heritage caution us against extracting a principle from the Bible, including the prophetic principle, removing it from its concrete historical and social context, and applying it indiscriminately in other situations. In addition to Asian reappraisals, feminist scholars have also examined the prophetic tradition with reference to the suppression of goddess worship.[14] Jewish feminist Judith Plaskow examines the implications of a monotheistic understanding of God, the suppression of female images of the divine, and the fear of sexuality for a quest for feminist spirituality.[15] While the prophetic tradition has always been important in Third World theology, Song is right that the prophets' negative attitude toward other religions has contributed to the distrust of popular religion and an insensitivity to theological motifs expressed in other religious and cultural idioms.

Several biblical scholars from Asia have begun to apply the dialogical approach to the study of the Bible. Their scholarship focuses on the New Testament, particularly on the person and teachings of Paul. I shall give two examples from different contexts as illustration.

R. S. Sugirtharajah interprets Paul's spiritual experience on the road to Damascus from the religiously pluralistic context of the Indian subcontinent. Traditionally, there are two approaches to Paul's experience. The "conquest approach" sees Paul's experience in terms of conversion from Judaism to Christianity; "he is conquered by Christ and he is sent to conquer others for Christ."[16] The "reorientation approach" sees Paul as changing from one of the Jewish sects to another. Sugirtharajah argues that both these approaches are insensitive to people of other faiths. Instead, he opts for a dialogical approach, which "acknowledges the validity of the varied and diverse religious experiences of all people and rules out any exclusive claim to the truth by one religious tradition."[17] Sugirtharajah says Paul was proud of his Jewish heritage and did not use the vocabulary associated with conversion to describe his religious experience, which can be best described as a form of transformation—metamorphosis. He was brought to see new possibilities of relating to God through Jesus, who initiated a revitalization movement within his own Jewish tradition.[18]

Khiok-khng Yeo, who teaches biblical studies in Hong Kong, learns from Paul's handling of the issue of eating foods sacrificed to pagan gods (1 Cor. 8) one way to deal with ancestor worship in the Chinese context. Using a rhetorical approach, Yeo analyzes the social environment that gave rise to the controversy, Paul's audience, and his rhetorical techniques in argumentation. Yeo identifies Paul's audience as gnostic Christians, who believed that intuitive knowledge of God alone was necessary for salvation. Initially Paul argues that these gnostic Christians had some validity in their conviction that eating sacrificed foods did not really matter. Then at verse 10 Paul introduces an imaginary interlocutor to show the weakness of their argument, maintaining that knowledge alone does not guarantee salvation. Yeo argues that Paul's rhetorical style is dialogical: Paul creates a community discourse by first identifying with the dominant voice and then letting the people who were afraid to eat sacrificed foods speak indirectly through him. In this way Paul's rhetoric allowed all parties to talk and listen to one another. For Yeo, Paul's dialogical approach has hermeneutical implications for the context of Chinese ancestor worship. The fact that Paul did not simply condemn or support a view, engaging instead in an ongoing process of discourse and interaction in which all parties could be involved, offers us insights that can be appropriated in other situations.[19]

From a religiously pluralistic perspective, Asian theologians and biblical scholars explore the accommodations and tensions between Israel and her cultural and religious environment. An interfaith dialogical approach does not absolutize one tradition above all others. It sensitizes the reader to the multicultural and religious forces that shaped the biblical narrative and to the different perspectives embedded in the text, including those that were neither Jewish nor Christian, the viewpoints from which the biblical stories were told.

EXAMPLES OF MULTIFAITH HERMENEUTICS

In addition to reading the Bible from the perspective of interfaith dialogue, Asian theologians have also drawn upon the wisdom and resources of ancient Asian myths, scriptures, fables, and stories for new insights into how to interpret the Bible. Currently three approaches are used by Asian scholars. Some compare similar motifs through cross-textual studies in order to draw out hermeneutical implications. Others look at the Bible through the perspective of other religious traditions. Still others discern biblical and theological insights in people's stories, myths, and legends.

Archie Lee in Hong Kong has written a number of essays comparing the creation myths in Genesis with the creation stories of China.[20] In the Chinese stories human beings are created by a female figure, Nüwa; she makes them out of yellow earth and mud. In addition, it is she who restores the social and cosmic order when the pillars of heaven are destroyed and water covers the whole earth. Nüwa is also honored as the matchmaker who institutes the marriage rite and is patroness of matrimony. Lee points out these motifs—creation of human beings from the earth, restoration of order out of chaos, and the ordination of marriage to continue the human race—are found also in the Genesis story. But there are differences in the two stories: Nüwa, as a human being, was raised to the highest heaven and transformed into a divinity in ancient China. In traditional Chinese thinking, divine and human beings exist in a continuum and are not sharply divided into two separate realms. In the Genesis story the creator exists separate from all creation.[21]

Lee raises several hermeneutical questions at the end of his study. He emphasizes that creation stories, which give an account of the creation of both human beings and the order of the universe, can be found in most cultures. Biblical scholars can look beyond Ancient Near Eastern myths for comparison. In comparing the motifs found in creation stories Lee reminds us not to gloss over the differences, because these provide insights into the different worldviews. Asian cultural resources, if taken seriously, will demand that Asian theologians reexamine Christian doctrines and become more open to other theological articulations.[22]

Another example of cross-cultural textual studies is George M. Soares-Prabhu's comparison of Jesus' Great Commission (Matt. 28:16-20) and a "mission command" given by the Buddha to his followers in the Mahavagga, a section of the Vinaya texts of the Pali canon. Given at the end of Jesus' life, the Great Commission concludes the Gospel of Matthew; the mission command is one of the incidents in a crucial period of the life of the Enlightened One. Soares-Prabhu notes that the two commands have a similar form: the grounding of the mission in the authority of the sender, the charge of the mission to teach others, and the return to the sender whose presence accompanies those who are sent. But a careful comparative study shows differences in the content as well: the Buddhist command emphasizes that followers must have religious experiences of enlightenment themselves before they can proclaim the message. Further, the aim of the Buddhist mission has a much broader scope: seeking welfare not only for humankind but also for all other beings in the world. Soares-Prabhu notes that the christological focus of the Great Commission and its missiological overtones sometimes lead to triumphalism and the self-aggrandizement of those who carry out the mission. A comparative study with the Buddhist text draws our attention to these implicit elements in the Great Commission and in other parts of the gospel that might otherwise be overlooked.[23]

These two studies differ from the earlier attempts at indigenization in that they are not missiological in nature. The comparison with traditional myths and scripture in Asia is not meant to prove that Christianity is compatible with indigenous tradition but aims at a "wider intertextuality"[24] and a fruitful and continuous cross-cultural dialogue. As Archie Lee says:

> Cross-textual hermeneutics gives due attention to the two texts at our disposal for doing theology. It is imperative that the Biblical text (text A) has to be interpreted in our own context in constant interpenetration and interaction with our cultural-religious texts (text B).[25]

In earlier times the similarities between the two texts would be highlighted, and when differences occurred, the Bible was invariably taken as the norm. But in these more recent attempts both similarities and differences are noted. The differences can be used to amplify certain dimensions of the biblical text or to bring to the surface divergences in the religious worldviews shaping the texts. The tensions between the two texts call for more in-depth dialogue and reexamination of Christian doctrines.

A second approach is to look at the Bible through the perspective of people of other faiths. Rooted deeply in his Hindu spirituality, Mohandas Gandhi was fascinated by Jesus' teaching, especially the Sermon on the Mount. Although he could not embrace the Christian belief that Jesus is the only begotten Son of God, he regarded Jesus as one of the greatest teachers humanity has ever had.[26] He was impressed by Jesus' teaching of nonviolence and his reading of the gospels confirmed many of his own beliefs. He wrote:

My reading of [the Bible] has clearly confirmed the opinion derived
from a reading of the Hindu scriptures. Jesus mixed with the publicans
and the sinners neither as dependent nor as a patron. He mixed with
them to serve and to convert them to a life of truthfulness and purity.
But he wiped the dust off his feet of those places which did not listen to
his word. . . . Enlightened noncooperation is the expression of anguished
love.[27]

Gandhi said the West misunderstood Jesus and mistook his bold and brave
resistance for passive resistance. For Gandhi, Jesus was "the most active re-
sister known perhaps to history."[28]

Another example is a fascinating study of "I" in the words of Jesus by a
Japanese Buddhist scholar, Seiichi Yagi.[29] Yagi notes that the new quest for
the historical Jesus in the 1950s and 1960s focused on the messianic consciousness of Jesus; that is, whether or not Jesus was conscious of himself as
the Son of Man. The concern was both christological and soteriological. Yagi,
a Buddhist, is more interested in what the self-consciousness of Jesus reveals
to us about the structure of human existence. In other words, his starting point
is anthropological. Using the Buddhist understanding of non-duality, Yagi
argues that the "I" of Jesus has two centers: the ultimate subject (God) and
the empirical ego (the man Jesus). But in Jesus the two centers are united, so
that when Jesus says, "I say to you," there is both the human Jesus speaking
as well as the ultimate subject speaking through him. In Jesus the divine and
the human are at the same time one and two. The double structure of human
existence is also seen in Paul when he says, "I . . . not I, but the grace of God."
However, human beings are not conscious of the divine nature in themselves and
need awakening or enlightenment. Jesus, revealing the double nature of humanity, becomes the object of faith in Christianity. For Yagi, the understanding that
the divine is in each of us is not found in Christianity alone. Mahayana Buddhism
also teaches that every living being has a buddha-nature, and so we need not
speak of an exclusive revelation in Christ.

Looking at the Bible from the perspective of other faiths, Gandhi and Yagi
are not bound by the Christian framework when they read the Bible. They
treat the Bible as a religious resource to address issues common to all humankind or as a mirror offering a reflection of their own tradition. Gandhi highlighted the nonviolent ethics in the Sermon on the Mount and Jesus' radical
commandment of love. Yagi looks at Jesus' self-consciousness to understand
the structure of human existence, without subscribing to an exclusive
christology. Asian theologians can learn from these colleagues about several
things: 1) common issues that people of other faiths are interested in, so that
interfaith dialogue can be promoted, 2) the usefulness of other hermeneutical
methods when applied to the Bible, 3) hidden pre-understanding that we all
have when interpreting any text, and 4) common vision for a just, participa-
tory, and democratic Asia.

The third approach involves the use of Asian myths, stories, fables, and legends to do theology and to interpret biblical stories. In the past decade the Program for Theology and Cultures in Asia, under the guidance of C. S. Song, has held seminar-workshops to encourage the recovery of Asian cultural and spiritual resources for doing living theology in Asia. Several anthologies on various topics—such as "Doing Theology with Asian Folk Literature," "Doing Theology with People's Symbols and Images in Asia," "Doing Theologies with Stories of the Spirit's Movement in Asia"—have been published.[30]

Searching for a new beginning to do theology, these writings challenge the text-context interpretative mode in earlier attempts at indigenization. This old mode often assumed that once we know what a text meant in its original context, we can then employ the text to illuminate or give theological meanings to the Asian context.[31] The text itself was considered fixed, static, and given. More and more Asian theologians are aware that we need to relate our Asian context to the text as well, so that the context may illuminate the text.[32] In other words, the relation between the text and the theologian's context should not be one-dimensional, but dialogical.

In the past, indigenization focused on the relationship between Christianity and the classical or high culture of Asia, and the people's voices were often ignored. In sharp contrast, these newer writings take seriously the popular culture of the people—stories, fables, and legends passed on from generation to generation—because they provide rich resources for theological imagination. Not just a social category to be analyzed, the poor are people with rich cultures and histories. C. S. Song urges his Asian colleagues to discern the theological significance of popular culture and to learn from this new way to look at both the world and the Gospel. Song says we need to develop a "people hermeneutic," because, for him, the people are the clues to the real identity of Jesus. Jesus' story is the story of the people.[33]

People hermeneutics challenges the abstract and highly philosophical hermeneutics of the West, which is often alienated from life. People hermeneutics uses storytelling as a hermeneutical tool to understand both the Asian reality and the Bible. In doing so, it emphasizes the story character of the Bible and Jesus as a storyteller. No longer dictated by rules and norms superimposed from the outside, this approach represents a fresh beginning to understanding what the Bible has yet to disclose through the lived and living experiences of the peoples of Asia.[34] Because stories need to be told and retold, people hermeneutics is never fixed and final but always open to new possibilities.

I shall give two examples to illustrate this approach, one from Japan, the other from the Philippines. Yuko Yuasa uses stories in Japanese Noh drama to challenge the theme of sacrifice in the Bible.[35] Noh drama has its roots in popular performance rituals depicting the stories of the gods and ancestors before the ancient farming communities of Japan. In a Noh drama entitled *Motemezuka*, the maiden Unai was loved simultaneously by two men. If she married one of them, the other would be jealous and offended. In distress, she committed suicide by jumping into the River Ikuta. Yuasa places this story within the larger context of the tradition of female sacrifice in Japanese culture: the offering of women as sacrifice on behalf of the community, the demand that mothers should be self-sacrificing, and the discarding of old women when they are considered to have become burdens to society. She then questions the church's teaching on servanthood, especially when applied to women. Citing passages from the psalms and the gospels, she insists that God does not demand sacrifice but mercy and a chastened heart and she rasies the challenge that the religious ideals of servanthood and self-sacrifice, exemplified by the cross, have often been used to justify subordination of women.[36]

In another example Levi V. Oracion of the Philippines tells a myth based on indigenous beliefs prior to Spanish colonization of the Philippines.[37] On the island of Mindanao in the southern part of the Philippines people once lived peacefully in the highlands, but the life of the community was threatened suddenly by the arrival of several man-eating monsters, who plundered the land. Chief Indarapatra sent the warrior Sulayman to save the people from the monsters. Sulayman successfully conquered several monsters but was killed in the final combat. Indarapatra set out to find Sulayman and managed to revive him by pouring some magical water onto his dead body. Peace and order was restored, and the community lived happily afterward. Oracion uses this story to illustrate the suffering of innocent people living under evil conditions. For him, this affirmation of hope in spite of tragedy and evil and the conviction that freedom and peace will come after a long and bloody struggle can be compared to some of the notions in the Bible. Just like the resurrection of Christ, the hero's coming to life again is an acknowledgment that justice prevails over evil. Oracion concludes that in this mythical story many aspects are identifiable with the human cry and hope that we find in the pages of the Christian scriptures.

ISSUES IN MULTIFAITH HERMENEUTICS

Multifaith hermeneutics affirms that truth and wisdom are found not only in the Bible but also in the cultures, histories, and religions of other people. It challenges us to look at the biblical tradition from a much broader worldview and cultural framework. As D. Preman Niles from Sri Lanka writes:

It is not enough for Christian theology to work with a Mediterranean world view, reflected in the biblical world view, coupled with a modern western scientific world view. Other religious world views and their symbol systems also have to be taken into account.[38]

Learning to look at the Bible from other religious worldviews is a demanding task even for theologians in Asia, who live in a religiously pluralistic society. Until recently, there has not been a self-conscious and sustained effort to articulate a biblical hermeneutics from the Asian context. Although a few Asian theologians have discussed the ways people of other faiths have interpreted their scriptures, not much has been said about how to borrow the insights from Asian hermeneutical traditions to interpret the Bible.[39]

In fact, Asian theologians debate among themselves about how to assess their religious and cultural traditions. Some regard the Asian scriptures and hermeneutical traditions as important resources for a cross-cultural reading of the Bible. Others point to the failure of the earlier indigenization efforts, which tended to romanticize traditional Asian culture and to overlook present-day socio-political struggles. Focusing more on the culture of the oppressed, they are suspicious of an elitist tradition that often has served to provide rationalizations in support of the ruling class.[40]

I think that our response to the cultural past need not be either wholesale rejection or uncritical acceptance. In ignoring the hermeneutical traditions of Asia, Asian theologians cut themselves off from their very ancient intellectual heritage. Studying and writing commentaries on Asian scripture and classical texts have been an important part of intellectual life in Asia. The Asian cultural heritage includes voluminous glossaries, indexes, exegeses, and commentaries. Without learning Asian hermeneutical methods, Asian theologians cannot enter into dialogue with other Asian intellectuals and lack the critical tools to examine their own scriptural and cultural resources. More cross-cultural and comparative studies on exegesis, commentary, and hermeneutics are needed.[41]

Above all, we should guard against a simple polarization of high culture versus popular culture. The intellectual tradition in Asia should not be dismissed in a generalized way as working for the status quo. There are numerous instances of Asian intellectuals discovering new ideas and working for social reforms through the study of their scripture and classical texts. On the other hand, popular culture should not be romanticized. Not all of its elements are revolutionary in nature. We should emphasize those popular art forms and cultural expressions that reflect the reality of people's lives and articulate their aspirations. High culture and popular culture constantly interact with and borrow from one another. Critical evaluation of both is necessary. Theologians who are committed to learning from the poor should question the "elitist" assumption that the poor and oppressed are necessarily uneducated and do not share the cultural and religious orientation of the society at large.

A more nuanced understanding of the multilayered Asian culture does not dismiss the critical challenge of the poor to the religious and cultural traditions of Asia. Instead of assuming that any faith tradition is monolithic, we should be alert to the influences it has on people of different races, classes, and genders. Furthermore, we should expand the Asian hermeneutical tradition to include both the intellectual and written as well as the popular and oral. The influence and use of scripture in the life of the community—including liturgy, drama, song, and aesthetics—must also be taken into consideration. The dire poverty of Asia challenges any hermeneutics to integrate theory and praxis, and to move beyond seeking explanations to commitment to social transformation.

Multifaith hermeneutics heightens our consciousness of the hermeneutical assumptions underlying eastern and western traditions. We can explore these different assumptions by looking at the relation of hermeneutics to language and reality on the one hand, and history on the other. Paulos Gregorios, a prominent Eastern Orthodox theologian in India, once charged that European exegetes have often reduced the question "How do I perceive reality and how can I improve the way I perceive it?" to "What are the rules to interpret the Bible and how do I improve my way of interpreting the Bible?"[42] Gregorios's challenge reflects differences in the understanding of truth and hermeneutics, as Stanley J. Samartha observes:

> Asian religious traditions such as the Hindu and the Buddhist do not believe that one can develop a scriptural hermeneutic which will yield truth by itself. True knowledge is not the fruit of logical investigation or the exegesis of scriptures, but a transformation of the knowing subject.[43]

In many Asian traditions, the knower, the known, and knowledge are not clearly separated. Thus, only a person who has the religious experience or who has been transformed can have the authority to transmit knowledge to others. Hermeneutics has to do with much more than the study of a given text; it includes the perception of truth behind the text and the relation of the text to the ethos and practice of the religious community.

Since the Enlightenment the understanding of *reality* and *truth* in the West has been much influenced by an emerging historical consciousness. The Bible, treated as a document of the past, has been subjected to vigorous historical scrutiny. In some Asian countries intellectuals have raised similar questions about the historical truth of their ancient classics and documents. For example, Chinese scholars in the early twentieth century debated whether ancient traditions recorded in the classics should be considered myth or history.[44] But in other societies the question of historical truth is not an issue: "In the Hindu-Buddhist context, which speaks of an endless succession of aeons (yuga) or of evolutions and devolutions and the transitoriness of all things, historical thinking does not really make sense."[45] The meaning of events is not understood in terms of what they accomplish in the historical sense but in the impact they have on the whole cosmic order.

A multifaith approach to hermeneutics reveals also the divergent assumptions Asian theologians make when they relate the biblical story to the Asian story. The belief that the Asian story is a forerunner or a preparation for the Gospel has largely been rejected because it still assumes the missionary approach. Many Asian theologians do not think the biblical story is a fulfillment of or superior to the Asian story. But they do differ in their opinions about the interaction of the two stories.

C. S. Song insists that Asian stories are resources to do theology because God is present in them and speaks through them. He refuses to separate context from revelation and emphasizes that "revelation runs into context and context runs into revelation."[46] His theological writings weave together the story of the Bible and the Asian story through a creative and artful transposition. In retelling both the biblical and the Asian stories Song discerns theological meanings in stories and myths arising out of a non-Christian context and reframes the biblical story in a way that is relevant to the Asian situation. Critical of abstract philosophical systems—both of Asia and of the West—Song proposes storytelling as a theological style. His work shows characteristics of oral hermeneutics: interweaving of stories, additive plot, and appeal to the subjective response of readers.

In contrast, Suh Nam Dong from Korea respects the boundaries of Asian stories more than Song does. He warns that Asian stories should not be baptized, or christianized, without allowing them to speak on their own terms. These stories sometimes challenge the biblical story and should not be simply integrated into the Christian narrative. Furthermore, Suh stresses that the Asian stories have their historical context and should not be used apolitically to express theological insights. When reading the biblical story Suh is more attentive to the socio-historical setting than Song.[47]

While Suh underscores the relationship between story and history, his Indian colleagues focus on the different worldviews the stories reveal. Instead of looking for differences between the biblical story and the Asian story, they search for points of contact and complementarity. Influenced more by a cosmological perspective, they try to find a broader vision to see the interrelationship of the two. Francis D'Sa writes:

> One will seek an organic and harmonious integration of all complementary perspectives; one will want to find out the interrelationship between them and the reasons for their differences. Certain aspects will be enhanced by one perspective but certain others pushed into the background. Perhaps this enhanced aspect will challenge the other perspectives to search for less prominent details which have been totally overlooked or neglected.[48]

The differences among Asian theologians reflect not only their theological positions but also the ways their thinking is shaped by their own cultures and worldviews. The interaction between the biblical story and the Asian story remains open-ended, depending on changing circumstances.

Women who participate in the work of multifaith hermeneutics may see the issues more from the perspective of gender. For example, they insist that women's stories be included among the people's stories. They lift up stories women have told that give meaning to their lives and empower them in their

struggle against male oppression. Choi Man Ja from Korea examines the female images of God in the myths and stories of Korean shamanism, an indigenous tradition that sustains the poor people.[49] Aruna Gnanadason tells stories about the Hindu goddess Shakti, who symbolizes the creative power and
divine force of feminine energy.[50] Both women emphasize the use of these
stories in doing feminist theology in Asia.

Asian women theologians are more conscious than their male colleagues
of the androcentric elements within the Asian cultural heritages. Gnanadason
says Asian women must adopt a hermeneutics of suspicion in the face of "traditional spiritualities, of traditional interpretations of scriptures and even of
traditional understandings and analysis of society."[51] Asian women are painfully aware that many Asian religious traditions have reinforced male dominance in the society. The statement of the first Asian women's consultation on
interfaith dialogue in 1989 states: "As a result of religious discrimination,
women of all religions continue to be marginalized and discriminated against
at the societal level. And societal prejudices in turn influence religion in a
cyclic fashion."[52]

In addition, Asian women theologians are critical of the androcentric elements in the Bible and the suppression of women's stories and voices. C. S.
Song finds the story of the cross and resurrection of Jesus pivotal for his
creative theological reimaging. *Minjung* theologians in Korea use the story of
the *minjung* of the Bible as a hermeneutical key. Indian male theologians focus on the cosmic dimension of the Gospel and the cosmic Christ. But Asian
women find that biblical stories, told mostly from an androcentric point of
view, cannot be readily related to their experiences. Multifaith hermeneutics
for women, therefore, is not characterized by a hermeneutics of consent to
the biblical story and the Asian story but rather a process of double
hermeneutics of suspicion and reclamation.

Finally, Asian women theologians are more conscious of the fluidity of
different traditions in women's spirituality. As Chung Hyun Kyung has observed: "In their struggle for survival and liberation in this unjust, women-
hating world, poor Asian women have approached many different religious
sources for sustenance and empowerment."[53] In Chung's presentation at
Canberra, she performed a shamanistic ritual and used neo-Confucian and
Buddhist concepts to interpret the renewal of the Holy Spirit. Multifaith
hermeneutics, therefore, takes place not only between people of different faiths
but also within the spiritual life of many Asian women. Less concerned with
the boundary between orthodoxy and heterodoxy, many women have created
religious meanings in their dialogical appropriation of different traditions.

6

WOMAN, DOGS, AND CRUMBS

Constructing a Postcolonial Discourse

From there he set out and went away to the region of Tyre. He entered a house and did not want anyone to know he was there. Yet he could not escape notice, but a woman whose little daughter had an unclean spirit immediately heard about him, and she came and bowed down at his feet. Now the woman was a Gentile, of Syrophoenician origin. She begged him to cast the demon out of her daughter. And he said to her, "Let the children be fed first, for it is not fair to take the children's food and throw it to the dogs." But she answered him, "Yes, Lord, even the dogs under the table eat the children's crumbs." Then he said to her, "For saying that, you may go—the demon has left your daughter." So she went home, found the child lying on the bed, and the demon gone (Mark 7:24-30).

The story of the Syrophoenician woman has always fascinated me because she was a pagan and a Gentile woman. Some scholars have noted that she is the only example in Mark (and perhaps in Matthew) of a healed patient who is definitely a Gentile pagan.[1] In reading her story I would like to learn more about how a Gentile pagan woman functions rhetorically in the biblical narrative. Like much of the information we have about Third World women, our knowledge of this Gentile woman does not come directly from her. Told in the Gospels of Mark (7:24-30) and Matthew (15:21-28) as part of the Christian canonical text, through the centuries her story has not been interpreted by her own people—Syrian-Phoenicians who belonged to other faiths—but by Christians, who appropriated her for their own specific purposes.

The story of the Syrophoenician woman has special significance for people in the non-biblical world. The encounter of this woman with Jesus has been taken by the Church as a basis for mission to the Gentiles. Christian missionaries often regarded people in Asia and in other parts of the world who belonged to other faith traditions as "pagans" or "heathens." Such derogatory labels are still used by the Religious Right to justify their aggressive and high-tech attempts to convert people in the Third World. The story of the Syrophoenician woman brings into sharp focus the complex issues of the relationship among different racial and ethnic groups, the interaction between men and women, cultural imperialism, and colonization.

In doing research on this relatively short story I have become aware of the various layers of traditions embedded in the two gospel stories, as well as the competing claims of diverging models of interpretations. Our backgrounds and interests often shape the ways we formulate questions, gather and interpret data, and choose reading strategies to approach the text. My guiding questions in approaching the Syrophoenician woman's story are as follows: How does an unknown Gentile woman's story serve to legitimate the Gentile mission of the Christian Church? How can we interpret the story in such a way as to further the liberation of Third World women? In our postcolonial world, how can we reread the story so that we can respect one another as persons of different gender, race, religion, and social origin?

A GENTILE WOMAN IN THE MASTER DISCOURSE

In her literary and cultural studies Gayatri Chakravorty Spivak raises the crucial problem of "master discourse and native informants" in the presentation of colonized subjects in western discourse. By "master discourse," Spivak means the attempt to represent or construct the subject of the marginalized Other through discursive practices.[2] She challenges the power dynamics underlying how colonized people are inscribed in the text and how they are consigned to signify the Other in history. Although her observations are based on literature produced during the era of imperialism, her critical insights are helpful for understanding how a Gentile woman's story is presented in a Christian text and subsequently appropriated in the history of her story's reception.

The use of master discourse is double-edged in its application to the Gentile woman's story. First, her story is available to us through the master discourse of the gospels—the carefully constructed narrative texts of Mark and Matthew. Second, biblical scholars, following Bultmann, have classified her story, not as a miracle story, but as a pronouncement story, that is, a story that contains sayings of Jesus.[3] In other words, the story is understood by many as framed within the context of the discourse of the master, Jesus. Not surprisingly, much of traditional scholarship has focused on what can be learned about Jesus from this story: historical facts about his life, authenticity of his sayings, his attitude toward Gentiles, and his understanding of his own mission.

I am interested, however, in the rhetorical function of the Gentile woman's story. The biblical text is not a historical record of what actually happened between a woman and Jesus, but a literary construction by means of which the author seeks to attain certain rhetorical goals. Following Mieke Bal, I do not see biblical text "as a transparent, immaterial medium, a window through which we can get a glimpse of reality" but as "a figuration of the reality that brought it forth and to which it responded."[4] A postcolonial interpretation cannot ignore the social and historical forces that undergirded the production and transmission of the text. A critical analysis of the Gentile woman's story must take into consideration the hierarchy of subject and object inscribed in the text, the circumstances that brought it forth, and the rhetorical function it performs.

How Is the Woman Represented?

Mieke Bal's narratological model of analysis helps us to see clearly the hierarchy of subject and object in the gospels' presentation of the woman. To every text, Bal suggests, we must pose three questions: who speaks (language), who focalizes (vision), and who acts (action).[5] We shall ask first who it is that focalizes and acts. Below we shall analyze in detail the language of the pericope. In both Mark and Matthew the focalizer is the narrator. The narrator in Mark sets the stage by describing how the woman enters the house and bows before Jesus. The narrator is more lively in Matthew and invites the reader to focalize with him: "Behold a Canaanite woman from that region came out" (v. 22, RSV). In both cases the woman is portrayed as an object to be seen and displayed.

In the Markan account the woman acts, but in a constrained way. In the first action, it is she who comes and bows down before Jesus. In the second action, she is not the one who accomplishes the central act, namely, healing the daughter. Instead, she is a spectator, witnessing a miracle being performed by someone else. In the Matthean account the woman is accorded more action: she comes out shouting, continues to shout, and then kneels before Jesus. In both stories her body language—bowing and kneeling—demonstrates clearly her subordinate position in respect to Jesus. According to the customs of the time, "falling at the feet of another is the gesture of a client seeking a favor from a patron or broker."[6]

In Mark the woman's request that Jesus heal her daughter is reported indirectly by the narrator (v. 26). In contrast, in Matthew she is the first woman given a voice, and so we need to pay attention to the conditions that allow a woman to speak. The woman makes three petitions in direct speech (vv. 22, 25, 27). As a speaking subject she commands neither authority nor respect. She bows or kneels down before Jesus to ask for a favor, and then she is dismissed by the disciples. At first Jesus ignores her, and when he does answer, his reply sounds aloof, even rude.

Although given a voice, the woman's speech is clearly framed in a christocentric and androcentric discourse. In Matthew she addresses Jesus as Son of David (v. 22) to remind the reader of the genealogy at the beginning of the gospel (1:1-17). This patrilineal genealogy establishes Jesus' identity as the Christ, the son of Abraham, and the son of David.[7] She also uses the title

Lord to address Jesus, which actually reflects the christological thinking in the early Christian community.

Her response to Jesus—"Yes, Lord, even the dogs under the table eat the children's crumbs"—is neither confrontational nor argumentative. As David Rhoads observes: "As an inferior, the woman's response honors all that he says in his rejection and says nothing to contradict or shame him. She calls him 'lord,' recognizing his right to accept or reject her request."[8] Her speech displays the unequal positions of women and men in patriarchal society. According to Deborah Tannen, women and men exist in different worlds and their speech reflects the asymmetry of their positions in society. Men are more status conscious, Tannen says. Their "conversations are negotiations in which people try to achieve and maintain the upper hand if they can, and protect themselves from others' attempts to put them down."[9] In contrast, women's "conversations are negotiations for closeness in which people try to seek and give confirmation and support, and to reach consensus."[10] In the dialogue in Matthew the disciples and Jesus are more concerned with what Jesus, given his status, should or should not do. The woman, though denigrated by Jesus, speaks in a supportive and affirmative way, for she is concerned with maintaining the relationship.

When we compare her story with that of the Roman centurion in Matthew (8:5-13), a story that likewise involves a Gentile asking for healing, the different positions of the speaking subjects can be seen clearly. In the earlier episode the Roman centurion speaks with authority and his speech is framed as a man-to-man conversation: he talks about his own status and authority as an officer, and he is concerned that Jesus need not lower his status by entering his home. Furthermore, in that story Jesus responds immediately to the request by saying that he will go and heal the man's servant. Compared to the story of the centurion, the speech of the Syrophoenician woman is obviously constructed to express the asymmetry of status and speech of the two sexes.

What Does the Syrophoenician Woman Signify?

The relatively short story consists of a dense web of significations: Jewish homeland/foreign lands, inside/outside the house, Jews/Gentiles, cleanliness/uncleanliness, children/dogs, woman/disciples, and faithful/unfaithful. As a signifier of cultural, social, gender, and ethnic differences, the Syrophoenician is needed in the master discourse to name and display sameness and difference.[11]

The region of Tyre and Sidon, where Jesus meets the woman, belongs to foreign lands, in contrast to Galilee and Judea, the Jewish homeland. Scholars have raised the question whether Jesus actually traveled to the area of Tyre and Sidon, because the route does not quite fit what we know of Jesus' itinerary.[12] In Mark the woman enters the house where Jesus is staying, whereas in Matthew Jesus is outside in a public place together with his disciples. Elaine Mary Wainwright suggests that Matthew may want to direct the readers' attention away from the household of believers to those outside, waiting to get in.[13]

From the Jewish perspective the woman is an unclean Gentile, stigmatized further by a daughter who is possessed by an evil spirit. Though helpless with respect to her daughter's illness, the woman is not deprived of basic needs. Burton L. Mack observes that the people in the miracle stories do not constitute "a profile of average poor. . . . Marginality is more a matter of social stigma than poverty and oppression."[14] The woman is marginalized as a woman and as a Gentile, but she is Greek-speaking and from the urban class. As an outsider she stands simultaneously at the boundaries of the privileged and the marginalized.

Scholars point out that the reference to Gentiles as "dogs" is probably taken out of a Jewish maxim or proverb. In the story the Jews are the children, welcome to the table fellowship to partake of the bread, whereas the Gentiles are the dogs, excluded from the household of God. Since in this saying Jesus appears rude and offensive, scholars have proposed different ways to soften his harsh remark. Origen and others have suggested that Jesus means a little puppy, a pet that shares the house with children.[15] Francis Dufton makes the further distinction that Jesus refers to the "dogs outside," while the woman means the "dogs inside."[16]

The Matthean story includes the disciples, who ask Jesus to send the woman away. The disciples, who are supposed to be the insiders, fail to understand the purpose of Jesus' mission and present barriers for the woman. The negative portrayal of the disciples, several scholars have noted, is a literary and rhetorical devise to highlight the reversal of roles: the disciples lack faith, whereas faith is exhibited in the least expected place, by a Gentile woman.[17] This role reversal complicates the demarcation of the Other and the same in the biblical narrative. It raises numerous questions: Should we treat the Other as the same, include the Other in the same, or displace the same with the Other?

The Function of the Story in the Gospels

The story occupies a pivotal position in the narratives of both Mark and Matthew. According to Mary Ann Tolbert the story is the middle of three healing stories (6:53-56, 7:24-30, 7:31-37), that is, between the feeding of five thousand (6:35-44) and the feeding of four thousand (8:1-10).[18] With respect to Matthew, Janice Capel Anderson finds the story of the Syrophoenician or Canaanite woman at the center of a chiastic structure: two blind men (9:27-31), the sign of Jonah (12:38-42), the feeding of five thousand (14:13-21), the Canaanite woman (15:22-28), the feeding of four thousand (15:30-38), the sign of Jonah (16:1-4), and two blind men (20:29-34).[19]

Many scholars believe that the story has undergone stages of development and reflects uneasy tensions between Jews and the Gentiles in the early Christian community. T. A. Burkill, for example, has traced the different phases of the story's development in Mark and Matthew. At first membership in Jesus' congregations was limited to the Jews, and hence it was not good to take the children's bread and throw it to the dogs. Later it was understood that membership was based on faith in the Messiah, and both Jews and Gentiles could be admitted. In the third phase Jesus was said to travel to foreign lands himself. The bread of life, rejected by the Jews, was offered to the Gentiles. Matthew elaborates on Mark's story, adding other traditions he has received.[20]

Mark's original audience was primarily Gentile Christians. The story serves to justify the acceptance of Gentiles to the table fellowship of Jesus. Mark's anti-Jewish attitude appears in his portrayal of the bread of life being offered to the Gentiles after having been rejected by the Jews. Matthew builds on the story of Mark but adapts it to his Jewish audience by adding "Son of David" and attributing these words to Jesus: "I was sent only to the lost sheep of the house of Israel." In addition to the Jewish-Gentile conflict, feminist scholars have argued that the story also displays the tension brought about by women's participation in the early Christian community. Wainwright suggests that referring to the Gentile woman as a "dog" represents not only the degradation of her as a Gentile but also opposition to women's role in the liturgical and theological life of the church.[21] Jesus' affirmation of the woman may signal the legitimation of women's active role.

THE INTERSECTION OF ANTI-JUDAISM, SEXISM, AND COLONIALISM

The story of the Syrophoenician woman has been appropriated for various purposes in different periods. My point of departure is to investigate the intersection of anti-Judaism, sexism, and colonialism in the history of interpretation of this story.

Most interpreters of this story follow the salvation history model. Those who adhere to this model argue that the Gentile woman's story is included in the gospels to provide legitimation for admitting Gentiles into the Christian community. In this way the mission to the Gentiles is traced back to the historical Jesus, who allegedly traveled to the foreign region of Tyre and Sidon. Although reluctant at first, Jesus heals the Gentile woman's daughter, showing that Gentiles could partake in the salvation promised by God. Thus, the story of the Gentile woman serves as a myth of the origin of the mission to the Gentiles.

The inclusion of Gentiles was not straightforward and without barriers, as reflected in the story. According to a form-critical study of the Markan passage, the structure follows a specific pattern: petition, difficulty, overcoming of the difficulty, and assurance. In Matthew the pattern is repeated several times so as to heighten the difficulty and introduce greater dramatic tension in the story.[22] The disciples become part of the barrier when they ask Jesus to send the woman away. Furthermore, as Antoinette Wire has suggested, the difficulty is more dramatic when the healer himself becomes the obstacle.[23]

Here it is Jesus who refuses to answer the petition or, when he does reply, gives an offensive answer.

The turning point happens when the Gentile woman makes the pivotal remark: "Yes, Lord, even the dogs under the table eat the children's crumbs." Traditionally, this statement has been interpreted to signify both the woman's faith and her humility.[24] The harsh remark of Jesus is understood to test the faith of the woman. Although she is sharply attacked when Jesus calls her a dog, the woman persists until Jesus is compelled to hear her plea and praise her faith. She humbles herself and evokes the image of a "devoted dog" in her reply. The unequal subject positions of Jesus and the woman in the story are re-inscribed as offering a model of Christian virtue.

According to the salvation history scheme, salvation is first offered to the Jews, and once they reject it, the blessing is offered to the Gentiles. The Gentiles displace the Jews as the children of God, and the Jews become the "dogs," in an ironic turn of events. The salvation history scheme is clearly anti-Jewish and has been used to justify the persecution of Jews.

Furthermore, the strategy of displacement appears repeatedly in the history of this story's interpretation.[25] Martin Luther, for example, refers to the Gentile woman's story numerous times in his writings. The woman's faith, humility, and her identity as a Gentile were given new meanings during a critical time when Luther argued for the legitimation of a new Christian community. In his controversy with the Roman church, Luther emphasized that faith was the requirement for membership in the church. He contrasted the faith of the Gentile woman with that of Jacob, who wrestled with God, was given a new name, and later became the figure of a new community with a new relationship with God (Gen. 32:28).[26] He referred many times to Jesus' praise of the woman. He said the woman knocks and pounds the door so long that "Christ is compelled to yield and listen to her and to praise her faith and perseverance."[27]

The woman's humility and "contrite conscience" took on political overtones in Luther's argument with the pope and the Roman church. For Luther, humility opened the door for mercy because human beings could not boast their own righteousness before God. Luther commended the Gentile woman for not refusing to be a dog in God's house so that she could at least eat the crumbs.[28] Dogs, for Luther, were unclean animals and the lowest in value.[29] In contrast to the humility of the Gentile woman, the pope and the papists were proud, as if they knew all the truth and held the keys to heaven. In his trials and tests Luther took comfort that "solace has been promised to the contrite, hope to the despairing, and heaven to those who have been put into hell."[30]

Luther also read the acceptance of the Gentiles and the rejection of the Jews as metaphors for the acceptance of the fellowship of true believers and the rejection of the Roman church. Luther displayed his anti-Judaism when he wrote that the Jews were given the promise of God, but they were so arrogant and ungodly that they turned against God. As a result, God's mercy was open to the Gentiles. Similarly, Luther concluded that the promise to the Roman church was withdrawn because of its disbelief and pride. In so doing, Luther replaced and appropriated the "Gentile" identity for his own purpose:

> We are the guests and strangers who have come to the children's table by grace and without any promise. We should, indeed, humbly thank God and, like the Gentile woman, have no higher wish than to be the little dogs that gather the crumbs falling from their masters' table (Matt. 15:27).[31]

Later, when the Gospel was brought to interact with other cultures in Asia, anti-Judaism and sexism further intersected with colonialism in the interpretation of this story. First, the salvation history motif was further elaborated with the result that the faith and humility of the Syrophoenician woman served as a model not only for Christians, but also for "heathens," to ease the spread of colonialism and imperialism. Just like the Gentile woman, colonized peoples were expected to be as subservient, obedient, and loyal as a "devoted dog." As Ashis Nandy has shown, political and socio-economic dominance in colonial discourse is often symbolized by the dominance of men over women.[32] In a double displacement Christianity was understood to supersede Judaism as the true religion and to need to be exported all over the world, conquering peoples and displacing other religious traditions in the name of Christ.

Second, in order to appeal to the female audience, missionaries highlighted Jesus' love and care for women in dire need. In a religious tract written in 1871 by a missionary in China, the identity of the Gentile woman as a mother with a needy daughter is emphasized so that the audience can identify with her. The fact that Jesus first ignores her and is rude in his answer is not mentioned.[33] The interpretation of this story must be seen within the larger context of the discussion of Jesus' relationship with women in missionary discourse. Many women missionaries, who came from evangelical backgrounds, had a strong conviction that their lives were changed by Jesus, prompting them to go into the mission fields to uplift their "heathen" sisters. They contrasted Jesus' attitude toward women and his relationship with women with the understanding of womanhood in non-Christian cultures. Jesus' respecting his mother, teaching religious truths to women, healing women from sickness, showing compassion to widows and the needy, and appearing to Mary Magdalene after his resurrection were stressed.[34]

Jesus' relationship to women was often cited by missionaries as an example that Christianity accorded a higher status to women, while non-Christian cultures were seen as inferior and patriarchal, and the subordination of women was taken as one sign or manifestation of this inferiority. Such beliefs could be used to justify the ecclesial interest of Christian mission and the ethnocentrism of the West.[35] Furthermore, the assumption that Christians have a superior understanding of womanhood is anti-Jewish when Jesus' attitude toward women is contrasted with Judaism, which is condemned as irredeemably patriarchal. As Jewish theologian Judith Plaskow says: "It is thus possible for Christian feminists to use the same classical anti-Jewish framework to set up a new antithesis: Judaism equals sexism, while Christianity equals feminism."[36]

TOWARD A POSTCOLONIAL INTERPRETATION

A postcolonial interpretation must expose and investigate the intersection of anti-Judaism, sexism, and cultural and religious imperialism in the history of the text's interpretation. We cannot follow a single-axis approach, one that separates race, gender, class, and culture from one another. In other words, we must adopt a multiaxial frame of reference and examine the story from a multidimensional perspective.

Anti-Judaism in Biblical Interpretation

I have made the connection between anti-Judaism and colonization in the history of interpreting the story. This raises critical methodological questions in biblical interpretation from a Third World perspective. Plaskow makes the distinction between anti-Judaism and anti-Semitism. She says this allows us to speak of the fact that people "who are not social or racial anti-Semites still make use of anti-Jewish literary and theological motifs."[37] Third World theologians have not spoken much on the issue of anti-Judaism in biblical interpretation, and more discussion is needed.

Some of these issues include the following: 1) In what way can we appropriate a Jewish story for our own situation? An obvious example is the Exodus story, which has often been lifted from the original Jewish context and adapted for use in liberation theologies. What are the ethical issues involved in such appropriation and are there limits to such adaptation? 2) How can we avoid anti-Judaism in our interpretations of the Christian canonical text? I have shown that the Syrophoenician story cannot be interpreted as proclaiming the universality of the Gospel or the inclusion of Gentiles in the kingdom of God, without attending to the issues of anti-Judaism and Christian imperialism. We must interpret the Christian canonical text with a critical awareness of the ways other faith traditions are portrayed. 3) How do we deal with the notion of difference as inscribed in the text? The narrator of the Syrophoenician woman's story assumes there are differences among people: Gentiles and Jews, women and men, unclean and clean. As noted by Renita J. Weems in her discussion of ideological difference in another biblical text: "The notion of differences between people is not challenged, but is simply inverted and coopted for his or her own purposes and for his or her own ideological interests."[38] As contemporary critics, we must challenge ideological construction of sameness and difference on the one hand, and respect diversity in terms of race, gender, class, culture, and religion on the other.

Reconstructing Women as Subject of History

In *Women and Jesus in Mark* Japanese feminist biblical scholar Hisako Kinukawa places the story of the Syrophoenician woman within the discussion of cultic purity and social separation in the cross-racial community in Mark. She emphasizes the subjectivity of the woman and her courageous act:

> It is the mother who has to face adverse circumstances and carve a way out. The woman who expected to be invisible becomes visible and acts; suppressing any feelings of fear and hesitation that she might have, she knows they have little to lose and they must gain life.[39]

For Kinukawa, the Gentile woman has created an opportunity for Jesus to cross the boundary, to allow himself to be "defiled," and to see the situation in a new way: "Jesus is motivated to act, inviting the Gentile, the socially outcast, the materially poor, the sick, the oppressed, and the rejected into God's community."[40] Similarly, Sharon H. Ringe says the Gentile woman's story has christological significance because of her gifts and ministries to Jesus. First, she bears witness to Jesus as a miracle worker and as one who can be won by persistence. Second, her sharp retort enables Jesus to see the situation differently and to enlarge his ministry. Jesus is helped by the least expected person: a Gentile, a woman, and a social outcast.[41]

In a retelling of the Matthean story by a group of women in India, the Syrophoenician woman was given a name, Miriam. When the male disciples try to stop her, Miriam insists without any inhibitions that she must see Jesus and argues boldly with the disciples. Finally, Miriam asks for the help of a woman disciple, who takes her to see Jesus. The story ends by saying that the Gentile woman changes the mind of Jesus:

> Miriam: Lord, your mother is her mother. We are a part of the human race. Please include us in your mission. Please heal my daughter.
>
> Jesus: Woman, you have great faith. You have given me a vision without limits. My message is for all peoples; your wish will come to pass. Your daughter will be free. Go in peace.[42]

While these interpretations stress the woman's role in changing the vision of Jesus, Elisabeth Schüssler Fiorenza credits her as a speaking subject and reconstructs her story within women's historical leadership during a transitional period of the early church.

> Although the Syro-Phoenician respects the primacy of the "children of Israel," she nevertheless makes a theological argument against limiting the Jesuanic inclusive table-community and discipleship of equals to Israel alone. That such a theological argument is placed in the mouth of

a woman gives us a clue to the historical leadership of women in opening up the Jesus movement to "Gentile sinners" (Gal. 2:15). The story of the Syro-Phoenician makes women's contribution to one of the most crucial transitions in early Christian beginnings historically visible.[43]

Respecting the Religious Tradition of the Woman

The Syrophoenician woman has been seen as the prototype of Gentile Christians, whose faith stands in sharp contrast to the Jews. Several Asian theologians, however, are conscious of the fact that the story has too often been read from a Christian point of view, creating difficulties in interfaith dialogue. Sugirtharajah objects to interpreting the pericope from the church's missiological point of view. Such a reading interprets the story in terms of the missionary enterprise of the early church or in terms of the authentic faith of the woman. He disagrees with these two readings, because "one reading tends to see any Hindu, Muslim, Buddhist or Sikh as a potential target for evangelization and absorption into the Christian community, while the other projects Judaism as a dead letter awash with legalism and ritualism. The problem with such ecclesiocentric reading of the pericope is that it deters any meaningful dialogue with members of other faiths."[44]

Sugirtharajah notes that in Mark Jesus does not comment on the woman's faith. The story belongs to the genre of "faith healing and miraculous cures."[45] The woman has come forward not because of a spiritual request but because of the reputation of Jesus as a healer. Jesus grants her request not because of her faith but because of her manner of speech. In Matthew, Jesus praises the woman's faith, but there is no suggestion that she then follows Jesus. After this one episode she vanishes from the scene. Sugirtharajah agrees with Ringe, who interprets the story as "the woman's ministry *to* Jesus by her 'faith'—a faith that is no doctrinal confession of his messianic identity, and no flattery of his apparently miraculous powers, but rather an act of trust, of engagement, risking everything."[46] In the encounter Jesus is reminded that God's hospitality is so great that it transcends national and racial boundaries. For Sugirtharajah, "It is the evangelizer who is evangelized now."[47]

Another interpretation by a group of Asian and Asian American women also respects the Syrophoenician woman as belonging to another faith tradition. It recognizes religious pluralism existing in Jesus' time, just as in Asia today. The woman in the story may have her own form of worship and pray to other gods and goddesses. Instead of assuming that she becomes a Christian, the story is retold as a powerful inquiry into the identity of this Jesus whom she encounters:

> Who? Jesus? Who is this Jesus?
> Is this Jesus that the rich worship?
> In the name of whom, the powerful nations "convert"
>   the world?

> Is it not true that the disciples chase the Canaanite
> woman away?
>
> Asian women have met another Jesus.
> They have found the Messiah among the *Minjung*.
> There, at the corner of the street, in the prison cell,
> in the vast exploited land, and in the people who
>   never lose hope.
> The Canaanite woman must have found the same
>   poor, lowly and ragged Jesus.[48]

Such a retelling challenges the way the Gentile woman is re-presented in the master discourse and the image of the colonial Christ as introduced by the missionaries and foreign oppressors. It also begins to envision who Jesus is for the suffering people of Asia.

The Other within the Other

The Syrophoenician woman's story has been interpreted as the acceptance of the Gentile into the household of God or as the inclusion of women into God's kingdom. People who have suffered from the pain of exclusion have used this text to speak of the inclusion of everybody in God's compassion and love. Our analysis raises the poignant question of what conditions are necessary for including the woman. Too often interpreters rush to baptize her as a Gentile Christian without acknowledging the different culture and religious tradition she represents. In addition, many women are troubled by the fact that the Syrophoenician woman has to bend down and beg for the crumbs.

In appropriating the Gentile woman's story for contemporary use we should guard against a simple and reductionist understanding of the Other. The woman is stigmatized because she is considered to be an unclean Gentile woman. But Gerd Theissen argues that she is a Hellenized Phoenician from the border of Tyre and Sidon. Knowledge of Greek language and culture suggests that she is educated and from the upper class. Relatively affluent, she belongs to the urban dwellers who oppress the people in the Galilean hinterland.[49] We may be tempted to identify with her Otherness as racial minority, as women, or as the contemporary marginalized, without recognizing our own privileges and our own potential to exploit others. The Other is never a homogeneous group; there is always the Other within the Other. In our interpretation of the Bible we must make visible the multiple interlocking layers of oppression and always remember to make room for the Other within the Other. In interpreting her story Asian feminist theologians are concerned about the multiply oppressed people in the Third World. In retelling the story they make visible the concrete intersection of sexism, economic injustice, political oppression, and militarism in Asian women's lives:

Yes, who is this Canaanite woman?
She is the woman down on the dirty road of Calcutta.
She is the mother of a political prisoner in Seoul.
She is the old garment factory worker in Hong Kong.
She is the mother whose daughter is a prostitute in
    Jakarta, Taipei or Chiang Mai.
She is also this survivor from Hiroshima.

. . . .

The woman is the poorest among the poor,
the oppressed among the oppressed,
she is at every corner of Asia,
and she fills the Third World.[50]

7

RACISM AND ETHNOCENTRISM IN FEMINIST BIBLICAL INTERPRETATION

The Bible emerged from the rich cultures of different races and peoples living in Palestine, Mesopotamia, Africa, and the Mediterranean world. In the history of the Christian Church, the Bible has largely been interpreted from a white, male, and clerical perspective. As a result, the subtleties of the historical encounter between different cultures, the politics of racial relations, and the hidden voices of women in the biblical account have been either overlooked or interpreted from a very biased standpoint. The Bible has been used to legitimize racism, sexism, and classism, as well as to condone colonialism and cultural imperialism.

This chapter examines the related issues of racism and ethnocentrism in feminist biblical interpretation. The questions of race and ethnic identity both in the diverse biblical accounts and in the politics of interpretation will be explored from a Third World women's perspective. The aim is to clarify how the Bible has been constantly used to oppress women, especially Third World women and minority women in the First World, and to demonstrate how these marginalized women can help to recover the liberating potential of the Bible for the salvation of all.

I would like to present ten theses to help us address racism and ethnocentrism in biblical interpretation. These theses were developed from a careful and attentive reading of the writings of Third World and African American female theologians, biblical scholars, and women in the church. My observations will be chiefly based on my experience as an Asian Christian theologian, drawing also on insights from conversations with women of color in professional gatherings, in the ecumenical movement, and in the Ecumenical Association of Third World Theologians.

Thesis 1: The politics of biblical authority must be carefully examined from a feminist liberationist perspective.

The Bible has been understood as one of the most important foundations of faith for the Christian Church. The authority of the Bible is based on the belief that it is the revealed Word of God. During the missionary era the Bible was introduced to peoples around the globe at the same time as their lands were taken from them. The introduction of Christianity as part of western culture was understood to be "the white man's burden" for the "uncivilized heathens." Centuries of colonial conquest and the recent Gulf War, legitimated by religious jargon from politicians, make it absolutely clear that an ethnocentric understanding of the Bible and biblical faith is fatal to the peaceful coexistence of peoples of different faiths.

The Bible is doubly problematic for Third World women, because it has been used not only to support aggressive acts against their cultures but also against them as women. In places such as the Philippines and in African societies such as Ghana, the biblical religion introduced by the colonizers challenged indigenous beliefs and communal living in which women enjoyed relatively higher status and more freedom. In other East Asian societies, such as in China and Korea, the androcentric elements of the Bible were used to reinforce patriarchy in church and society.

Third World women theologians have begun to reexamine the issue of biblical authority from their own reality. Biblical scholar Teresa Okure tries to distinguish timeless truth in the Bible from its cultural underpinnings. She writes: "Rereading the Bible as a patriarchal book demands that sustained efforts be made to discern between the divine and the human elements in it. For while the former embodies timeless truths for our salvation, the latter inculcates practices that are socioculturally conditioned, hence inapplicable universally."[1] Elsa Tamez, who teaches theology in Costa Rica, affirms that the central message is essentially liberating, although there are antifemale texts in the Bible. She goes a step further than Okure in saying that the "time has come to acknowledge that those biblical texts that reflect patriarchal culture and proclaim women's inferiority and their submission to men are not normative; neither are those texts that legitimize slavery normative."[2]

Mine is the most radical view. I grew up in the non-biblical culture of Asia, and I do not believe that we can abstractly speak about the divine elements or the central message of the Bible without historical specificity. I am also aware that the concept of the "authority of the Bible" has no meaning for—and might even sound offensive to—the majority of Asians, who are non-Christians. For me, the critical principle of interpretation lies not in the Bible itself but in the community of women and men who read the Bible and who, through their dialogical imagination, appropriate it for their own liberation.[3] The authority of the text and canon of the Bible must be thoroughly demystified and deconstructed so that the Bible cannot be continuously used against marginalized women.

Thesis 2: The historical-critical method of interpretation, which grew out of a Eurocentric culture, must be critically judged from the experiences of local interpretive communities.

The historical-critical method of biblical interpretation emerged from a particular religious and intellectual milieu in Europe. On the one hand, challenged by rationalism and humanism, there was a religious need in the wake of the Enlightenment to examine and critique the doctrinal use of the Bible by the church. On the other hand, biblical scholars lived in an intellectual climate with heightened historical consciousness. They shared a modern concept of history that was "the ideological product of an emergent bourgeois liberal society."[4] Since then the historical-critical method, considered to be fact-finding and value-free, has been taken as the standard for biblical scholarship.

The historical-critical method is perhaps the most suitable praxis for white, male, middle-class academics, because they alone can afford to be "impartial," which literally means "non-committed." Oppressed women and men of all colors find that the historical-critical method alone cannot help them to deal with the burning questions they face. Illiterate women in the Third World churches care more about daily survival than about the value of any critical method. For Third World and African American biblical scholars, the method is helpful, yet too limiting, because it does not allow certain questions to be raised or certain perspectives to be entertained.[5] Renita J. Weems powerfully points out that the negative result of the historical-critical method has been "to undermine marginalized reading communities by insisting that their questions and experiences are superfluous to Scripture and their interpretations illegitimate, because of their failure to remain objective."[6] The "aural hermeneutics" of African American women, about which Weems speaks, has no place in this method; the Gospel in Solentiname as told by the peasants of Nicaragua will be taken as interesting "stories," but not as biblical commentaries.[7]

Many Asian and indigenous Christians live in cultures that understand history and historiography in a totally different way. The Eurocentric positivist approach must not be taken as the sole norm for historical quest. The Bible is too important to be subjected to *only* one norm or model of interpretation. The fruits of the historical-critical method must be tested and challenged by local religious communities that are daily reading the Bible anew and that have tried to weave their own stories and struggles with the biblical narratives.

Thesis 3: It is not enough to tell the history of how white women have developed a feminist critique of the Bible without simultaneously telling the parallel story of women of color. Our common heritage is our shared power.

Many women trace the development of a feminist critique of the Bible to the nineteenth century, when the first wave of feminism in America raised the consciousness of women sitting in the pew. They recount the courageous remarks of Sarah Moore Grimké and hail the publication of *The Woman's Bible* by Elizabeth Cady Stanton as ground-breaking. While the contributions of these white forerunners must not be forgotten, we should remember that women of color during the same period also tried to look at the Bible through their own dark eyes.

The story of how the grandmother of Howard Thurman, Nancy Ambrose, a former slave, rejected the white minister's interpretation of slavery is of critical importance for African American women.[8] Similarly, Jarena Lee and Julia Foote, two preachers in the American Methodist Episcopal Church, have challenged Paul's teachings, which circumscribe women's roles. Jarena Lee's famous speech illustrates this very well:

> For as unseemly as it may appear now-a-days for a woman to preach, it should be remembered that nothing is impossible with God. And why should it be thought impossible, heterodox, or improper for a woman to preach? seeing the Saviour died for the woman as well as the man. If a man may preach, because the Saviour died for him, why not the woman? seeing he died for her also. Is he not a whole Saviour, instead of a half one?[9]

In nineteenth-century China a Christian woman, whose name has not been recorded by the missionary, used a pin to cut out those passages in her Bible in which Paul teaches that wives should be submissive to their husbands. At the turn of the century a medical doctor, Zhang Zhujun, reportedly the first Chinese woman to preach from the pulpit, challenged Paul's prescription that women should keep silence in church.[10] The stories of these and other women of color must be remembered and told so that our heritage of courageous women can expand to empower us in our present struggle.

Thesis 4: Feminist interpretation of the Bible must take into serious consideration simultaneously the multiple oppression of women in terms of class, gender, and race.

Feminist theorists have clearly demonstrated that women's experience is determined not by female biology alone but is largely shaped by powerful cultural and social forces. In other words, there is no such thing as "universal" women's experience. Patriarchy is experienced in varied ways according to different social and political situations. As Elisabeth Schüssler Fiorenza has rightly pointed out, patriarchy should not be construed as "a universal transcultural binary structure," but should be understood as "a historical political system of interlocking dominations."[11]

Women in biblical times were shaped by their particular race, class, and social location, just as women today are. Biblical women who were at the lowest stratum of society help us to understand the multiple oppression of women in a most vivid way. The story of Hagar, the Egyptian slave girl of Abram and Sarai, has been taken as paradigmatic to show the intersection of racism, classism, and sexism by women of color in different continents.

In the United States, where slavery was abolished only in the mid-nine-teenth century, the story of Hagar is especially poignant and relevant. Hagar was given by her mistress as a concubine to her husband, her body was sexu-ally exploited, and she was humiliated and ridiculed by her mistress. For Af-rican American women, whose ancestors were slaves and whose mothers and relatives have worked as domestics, the story of Hagar is just too familiar. "It is a story that also exposes the many hidden scars and ugly memories of the history of relationships between racial ethnic and white women in America."[12]

For Latin American women Hagar is "the woman who complicated the history of salvation." Elsa Tamez observes that people tend to focus on Deborah, Esther, Sarai, and Mary when speaking about women in the Bible; seldom do they talk about Hagar, who is a "negative model." Many Latin American women see in the Hagar story important parallels to the events in their own lives: extreme poverty forced her into slavery; abandoned by her husband she struggled as a single mother; and powerful people around her tried to erase her from historical memory. What is important, according to Tamez, is that God instilled hope in her, and it was this slave woman who gave God the name El-roi, that is "God who sees" (Gen. 16:13).[13]

For African women the Hagar story is read in a context where polygamy still exists. A foreigner and a slave, Hagar was not given the full status of a wife, because in Hebrew society she was not eligible. Both Hagar and Sarai were valued only as "containers" of Abram's seed in their society. For Musimbi R. A. Kanyoro of Kenya, Sarai "sees Hagar as an instrument for meeting her own needs—in today's idiom, one may say a disposable instrument. It is an issue of women struggling against each other in order to fulfill what society has designed for them."[14] For Anne Nasimiyu-Wasike, the stories of polyga-mous marriages in the Hebrew Scriptures bring out "the consequences of po-lygamous family life—for example, rivalries, jealousies, envies, favoritism, quarrels over inheritance, succession feuds, injustices, hatred, and murders. These realities are the experiences of African polygamous families as well."[15]

As an Asian, what interests me most in the Hagar story is how she con-ducted her life as she struggled to survive in a Hebrew family. Philo observed that Hagar was "an Egyptian by birth, but a Hebrew by her rule of life."[16] The removal of Hagar's own cultural identity and the imposition of a new one demonstrate a pattern that is familiar, not only to people under slavery, but also to the vast number of Third World people living for centuries under the threats of colonial and neocolonial powers.

From the above discussion it seems that African American women focus on Hagar as a slave woman, Latin Americans stress that she was poor, Afri-cans underscore the fate of Hagar in polygamy, and Asians emphasize her loss of cultural identity. Each group observes a certain analogy between the oppression of Hagar and their own situation. Third World women and minor-ity women who are under multiple oppression help us to look at the Bible from the underside, because as the contemporary oppressed, they are more likely to "make the analogy between their own experience and similar social relationships reproduced in the biblical texts."[17]

Thesis 5: Anti-Semitism in feminist interpretation must be condemned and the Hebrew Scriptures must be interpreted in solidarity with Jewish feminists.

The greatest irony in the history of biblical interpretation is that the Hebrew Scriptures have been appropriated as the Old Testament of the Christians and used against the Jews. The Holocaust should forever remind us how anti-Semitism led to the genocide of the Jews of Europe, the horrible human tragedy of the twentieth century. Christian feminists must deal honestly with the ethical issue of how to appropriate Jewish myths, stories, and scripture without repeating the mistakes of the past. Judith Plaskow, a Jewish feminist theologian, has cautioned Christians to guard against anti-Semitic prejudices in their interpretation of the life and significance of Jesus.[18]

Asian Christians have always been aware that the Hebrew Scriptures grew out of a culture fundamentally different from their own. Asians have their own religious classics, but they do not understand religious writings as "Torah" (or sacred teachings that represent divine revelation), as the Jews do. For me, the Hebrew Scriptures represent one story of the slaves' struggle for justice in Egypt, the tension in building a just and caring community, the fight of refugees for survival in Babylon, and the continual struggles of small ethnic minorities living among powerful nations. Instead of treating these writings as revelation from God, I understand them to be one significant religious resource of humankind illuminating the human capacity to love, to struggle, to repent, and to cry in joy.

Plaskow, in *Standing Again at Sinai*, has called for a reinterpretation of the concept of Torah, so that it will no longer be used as an androcentric text, shaping the sacred memory of the Jewish people. The Torah should be expanded, Plaskow says, to include Jewish women's words, teachings, and history. Her understanding of the Torah as "the partial record of the 'Godwrestling' of part of the Jewish people"[19] is very liberating and helpful not only for Jews but for Christians as well. It allows room for Christian feminists to discuss and critique patriarchal elements of the Hebrew Scriptures without being labeled anti-Semitic. But this feminist critique must be done in a spirit of solidarity with Jewish feminists, and not in spite of them.

Thesis 6: The Bible should not be used to oppress or discriminate against any race or ethnic people.

Besides oppressing the Jews, the Bible has been used to discriminate against other races and ethnic groups. The exclusion of the Other is closely connected to the concept of election. Cain Hope Felder, an African American biblical scholar, argues that the explicit concept of Yahweh's preference for Israel over other nations and peoples developed relatively late. It developed into a religious ideology only in the period of Deuteronomic history toward the end of the seventh century B.C.E. Even so, scholars have debated whether one should look at the election of Israel strictly from a racial and ethnic point of view or as a symbol of "universalism" that emphasizes Israel's role as service to the nations.[20]

Although there may be nuanced meanings in the Jewish understanding of election, Christians have taken over this concept indiscriminately to oppress the Jews, the blacks, and all Gentiles. The Jews, who are blamed for the death of Jesus, are said to have lost their status as the chosen people, which is taken over by the Christians. The blacks are discriminated against specifically because of their skin color. Such discrimination is traced back to the ancient myth of Noah's curse of Ham (that he and his descendants would be slaves) and the choice of his brothers. The Gentiles are despised because they worship other gods and it is assumed that, unless they are brought into the Christian fold, they have no hope of salvation. These forms of discrimination are all rooted in the politics of the Other, but there are also differences in their historical and cultural specificities.

African American scholars have identified four principal ways that the Bible has been used against black people. First, the curse of Ham has been used as a religious ideology to justify the fact that blacks are innately and permanently inferior. Treating black women and men as chattel was accepted as the necessary fulfillment of the curse.[21] Second, there is the politics of omission, which minimizes the significance of black presence in the Bible. For example, Clarice J. Martin has documented how the ethnicity of the Ethiopian convert (Acts 8:26-40) as a black-skinned person has been downplayed by exegetes.[22] Third, there is an anachronistic tendency to read back into the Bible racial relationships as we experience them in modern times. In actuality, the Bible contains many favorable references to black people, such as the allusion to the Ethiopian king Tirhakah, who, it was hoped, would save the Israelites from the Assyrians.[23] Fourth, the existence of slavery in biblical times was used as a rationalization for modern slavery. The fact that neither Jesus nor Paul openly opposed slavery has been used by white people to legitimize the enslavement of other races.

The Bible has also been used against those who stand outside the Jewish and Christian traditions. The condemnation of the cultures, religions, and peoples in ancient Canaan can be seen as a forerunner of discrimination against all peoples who do not share the beliefs of Jews or Christians. The Canaanites were portrayed as worshiping idols, as promiscuous, and as having a lower moral standard generally. The conquest of Canaan has often been seen from the perspective of the "chosen people" of Israel. Recently Naim Stifan Ateek, an Arab Palestinian Christian, has raised the pointed question: "How can the Old Testament be the Word of God in light of the Palestinian Christians' experience with its use to support Zionism?"[24] Similarly, Native Americans identify with the Canaanites, the people who inhabited the land "promised" to Moses and his followers. Robert Allen Warrior, a member of the Osage Nation of the American Indians, charges that even those articulating theologies of liberation often overlook the Canaanite side, especially those stories that "describe Yahweh's command to mercilessly annihilate the indigenous population."[25] He further argues that "the Canaanites should be at the center of Christian theological reflection and political action. They are the last remaining ignored voice in the text, except perhaps for the land itself."[26]

Thesis 7: The Bible is the product of complex interaction among many different cultures. Discovering the cultural dynamics shaping the biblical account opens new horizons to see how the Bible functions cross-culturally today.

The Jews and the early Christians lived among neighbors with different languages, cultural codes, thought patterns, and religious practices. The encounter between cultures in the Bible was never one-dimensional. It was often very complex and subtle, involving not only rejection and resistance but negotiation and adaptation as well. In the Hebrew Scriptures the Israelites were severely warned against interracial marriages and adopting the cults and practices of the Canaanites. Yet these warnings were repeatedly overlooked, indicating that it was often difficult to uphold one's cultural and religious purity in a pluralistic world.

In the New Testament the cross-cultural encounter was even more complicated as Christianity emerged out of Judaism in the Hellenistic world. According to Lamin Sanneh this historical development involved a dual process of relativization of the Judaic roots and the destigmatization of Gentile culture as a "natural extension of the life of the new religion."[27] A better understanding of this process will enable Third World Christians to grapple with the issues surrounding the process of translating the gospel message, religious syncretism, and the function of Christian symbolism in different cultural milieus.

Given this complex background, the stories of Jesus meeting Gentile women in the gospels are particularly illuminating. I shall return to Jesus' encounter with the Syrophoenician woman (Mark 7:24-30) as an example. The story has often been symbolically interpreted as the basis for the admission of the Gentiles into the Christian church. But a study of the cultural "worlds" in the border region between Tyre and Galilee reveals more subtle dynamics at work. According to Gerd Theissen, the Syrophoenician woman was a Hellenized Phoenician who belonged to the Greek-speaking upper class. In the story she runs into a Galilean prophet in the rural territory belonging to Tyre.[28] The meeting was between two persons of different cultures, religions, classes, and genders.

Biblical scholars in the past have emphasized the faith of the Gentile woman, which led to the healing of her daughter. For Theissen, the miracle did not "consist in healing someone far away, but in the overcoming of an equally divisive distance: the prejudice-based distance between nations and cultures." He credits the woman with the ability to break through the walls that divided peoples.[29] Third World women and minority women interpret this story not from a christocentric perspective but from the point of view of the Gentile woman, who is a multiply oppressed person. Rita Nakashima Brock, a Japanese American theologian, points out that the Syrophoenician woman shatters Jesus' view of religious exclusivity. "It is the courageous work of the 'other' that shatters his view of power and privilege. That courage challenges the structures of benign paternalism that would give Jesus the power from above to fix the power inequities involved."[30]

Even though the Syrophoenician woman belonged to the elite urban class that exploited the Galilean hinterland, she was despised by the Jews and oppressed as a woman. She took her Gentile and female identity seriously when she challenged Jesus. Women in the Third World must take their identities seriously too when appropriating the Bible in a cross-cultural context.

Thesis 8: The Bible must also be read from the perspective of other faith traditions. Multifaith hermeneutics looks at ourselves as others see us, so that we may be able to see ourselves more clearly.

Asian Christians live on a continent populated by adherents of all the major historical religions of humankind. For them, the central hermeneutical question is how to interpret the Bible for people of other faith traditions. In our modern world, religious pluralism is a phenomenon not restricted to Asia, but rather a growing reality in many parts of the world. Moreover, the Bible is not read solely by Christians. Therefore, biblical scholarship must be accountable to the wider human family and not limit its audience to Christians only. The development of a multifaith hermeneutics must be given more serious attention.

The first step toward a multifaith hermeneutics is to recognize that a majority of the world's peoples live in cultures not shaped by the biblical vision. Asia alone comprises more than half of the world's population, and the Christian population makes up less than 3 percent. People of other faiths have their own religious practices and sacred writings. The Confucian classics have been read and memorized for more than two thousand years by the Chinese, and the *Bhagavad Gita* is revered as the "supreme book for the knowledge of Truth"[31] by the Indians. While the issues of the authority and the canon of the Bible might be crucial for Christians, they seem parochial to the vast majority of humankind.

Living in our multifaith context, the Bible can be studied in comparison with other sacred writings to bring out common themes and divergent emphases. Kim Sung Hae, a Korean woman and a Roman Catholic nun, has compared the sages in the Confucian tradition to the wise men in the Hebrew Scriptures.[32] Others have compared the *Bhagavad Gita* with the New Testament and studied the wisdom of the Hebrew Scriptures in the context of world religions.[33] In addition to these more descriptive comparisons, the Bible can also be interpreted from another religious perspective. For example, Seiichi Yagi, a Japanese Buddhist, has examined the words of Jesus from a Buddhist perspective.[34] Gandhi has also helped us to look at the Bible through the eyes of his Hindu spirituality.

The most difficult task for multifaith hermeneutics is how to reinterpret the Bible after seeing it through the lens of other faith traditions. It requires intellectual humility and radical openness to divine disclosure in other faiths and cultures. Such *kenosis* and inclusivity demand radical changes in biblical scholarship, which can no longer be carried out in the same old manner, as if we have learned nothing from decades of religious dialogue. Biblical scholars bury their heads in the sand if they continue to study the Bible as if it were a book of the past, without bringing out its potential to address contemporary issues. At the same time, it must be recognized that the insights and wisdom found in the Bible are but one religious resource of humankind, and they must be shared, tested, and corrected in the wider community of the human family.

Thesis 9: Women under multiple oppression have multiple identities, and they help us to interpret the Bible in a multidimensional way.

Third World women and minority women emphasize the fact that they have multiple and simultaneous identities as women under multiple oppression. According to Renita J. Weems, African American women cannot afford to read the Bible simply with the eyes of an "oppressed" man, but have to negotiate their multiple identities when reading.[35] The same holds true for Third World women.

From her experience as an Asian American, Rita Nakashima Brock describes a person with multiple identities as one who has the capacity to search for multiple voices that affirm complex cultural meanings and identities, thereby creating a fluid, multilayered self. This fluid self has a "tribal consciousness" which is "a moving center, a flexible observer that listens, reflects, and chooses in a constantly shifting attunement to experiences and relationships." It is able to hold all the voices and examine each one. It seeks to construct meaning in a fragmented world, to experiment with different voices, and try out versions of the stories.[36]

We have already seen how these multiple identities are brought to bear in the interpretation of the Hagar story. Other examples elucidate the complexities involved when one identity is at odds with another in reading the Bible. The Syrophoenician woman would be a good model for Gentile Christian women because she dared to challenge the Jewish identity of Jesus. But she also belonged to the elite class. Ruth, the Moabite daughter-in-law of Naomi, could be considered a woman of great faith. But according to the custom at that time, she married Boaz, a kinsman of her husband, to maintain her husband's name on his inheritance. Such practice would be considered improper and unchaste according to Asian customs.

The multiple identities of women enable them to maintain a critical distance when reading the Bible. As oppressed women, they interpret the Bible differently from oppressed men. For example, in her study of the household codes in the New Testament, Clarice J. Martin asks, "Why is the African American interpretative tradition marked by a forceful critique and rejection of a literalist interpretation of the slave regulations in the *Haustafeln*, but not marked by an equally passionate critique and rejection of a literalist interpretation regarding the subordination of women to men in the *Haustafeln*?"[37] In Africa there are men who try to keep the polygamous tradition as "the touchstone of genuine indigenization" of Christianity into Africa. But many African women strongly object to polygamy based on their rereading of the biblical stories on polygamous marriages.[38]

The Bible itself is a document of multiplicity and plurality. Women with multiple identities appropriate it in a multidimensional and multilayered way. It is as if many mirrors with varied sizes and surfaces were assembled at an angle to one another, creating and reflecting images in different directions and proportions. There is infinite potential in such fascinating reading and rereading.

Thesis 10: Racism and ethnocentrism are issues for all biblical scholars and not for Third World women or minority women only. The politics of "difference" in biblical hermeneutics must be examined.

People sometimes ask African American women why they always dwell on the story of Hagar and do not talk about other women in the Bible, such as Mary, the mother of Jesus.[39] Similarly, Gentile women can be asked why they always talk about the Syrophoenician woman or the Samaritan woman at the well. This is a catch-22 question. If we do not focus on these multiply-oppressed women, we risk being accused of missing our "unique" contribution to biblical hermeneutics. If we focus on slave and Gentile women, people wonder whether our biblical scholarship is too narrow in scope.

Third World women and minority women focus on the multiple oppression of women in the Bible because these stories speak to their reality and shed light on their existence. But their concern is not limited to the texts on women, or on marginalized women in particular. They seek to use these specific texts to uncover the interlocking oppression of racism, classism, and sexism in the past and in the present, thereby helping all of us to liberate ourselves from bondage. They wish to develop a biblical hermeneutics that addresses the liberation of all peoples, not women alone. This concern should be shared by all biblical scholars, and men and women reading the Bible for insights. Everyone should participate in the search for a liberating hermeneutics from one's particular social and historical location, while listening to the voices of others. It is morally dubious and intellectually dishonest to wait until the most oppressed women speak out and then appropriate their ideas and insights for one's own consumption.

Studying the Bible with integrity is a radical demand. Many Third World Christians, both women and men, have given up their lives, suffered under torture, or spent years in jail, as they sought to live out what the Bible taught them. Their question for all of us is: What price have you paid in your study of the Bible?

Epilogue

(The following sermon was preached at the Middle Judicatory Educators Conference of the Presbyterian Church, U.S.A., held at Stony Point Center in New York in December 1991. The day before the sermon the play The Promised Land *by George Fishoff was performed. Some of the quotations in the sermon were taken from the lyrics of that play.)*

Last night I traveled to the Stony Point Center in the same van with the artists who performed *The Promised Land*. When they asked me what I was doing there, I answered: "You are going to perform *The Promised Land*; I am going to interpret it." I guess I was invited because I am not only a theologian, but also an artist. As artists, we work with a particular medium. For them, it is their voices and music. The medium of my art is storytelling. This morning I will retell the story of the promised land, while adding a few stories of my own. I invite you to think about your stories too.

When we do our Bible study, it is important for us first to ponder why we need to do it. What are the burning questions from our own experiences and from the world we live in? As an Asian woman my interpretation of the story's context may be very different from yours. I would like to share three stories from the past several years in my life, stories which made me return to the Bible to see what it had to say to me.

The first event took place on June 4, 1989, when the tanks rolled into Tiananmen Square, trampling the bodies of young students and workers who were holding a peaceful demonstration there. About two thousand to three thousand people died; some of their corpses were burnt and could never be recovered. Only their crooked and badly mangled bicycles remained. From that day on, my theology would never be the same.

The second story happened on January 15, 1991, when I sat glued to the television set in order to see whether or not the Gulf War finally would be launched. When the first bombs were dropped, I felt a deep sense of tragedy. It was as if we had not learned enough from the atrocities of Hiroshima and Vietnam. The war was not between Iraq, on the one hand, and the United States and her allies, on the other. It was a signal that human beings have the horrible power to wipe each other off the surface of the earth, yes, in a minute or more, as if playing video games. I could never read the Bible in the same way again.

Recently, I read Paul Monette's book *Borrowed Time: An AIDS Memoir.*[1] The book describes in vivid detail the pain Paul and his lover Roger had to face during the last nineteen months before Roger died of AIDS. I cried many times while reading that book not only because of the suffering they had to endure but also because of the love Paul and Roger felt for each other. I was angry and upset that it takes the tragic disease of AIDS to teach us human vulnerability as well as the human capacity for love and caring. Since then, I cannot read the Bible in the same way.

What is the promised land if it is not a symbol of hope? For Christians, as well as for Jews, the image of the promised land signals God's everlasting promise that suffering is not the end, because God acts in history to bring us salvation and deliverance. But my three stories raise new questions about this promise, which was first revealed to Abram and later became the most cherished tradition in Jewish memory.

In my first story about the Tiananmen Square massacre, the image of China as my own promised land was shattered. For a long time we, the people of Hong Kong, have been separated from our country. Since my childhood I have read poems and songs glorifying the mountains and rivers of our motherland. China appears in our dreams and symbolizes our deepest yearning. Now we are to return in 1997, but where is that promised land that we often dreamed about and longed to go back to?

The second story reminded me that I had always pushed aside the issue of nuclear threat as if it were an issue only for Americans and Soviet people, because they were the ones building up nuclear empires. But the Gulf War revealed that we are intimately related. Representatives from Britain came to Hong Kong, soliciting funds to support British involvement in the war. No one is clean anymore, and nobody can wash his or her hands of it. Much of our contemporary history is shared history. On December 7, 1991, American people commemorated the fiftieth anniversary of the attack on Pearl Harbor. But what about August 6, the date 200,000 died in Hiroshima in a couple of minutes? Where is our promised land when citizens of powerful nations cannot stop their countries from going to war and citizens of smaller nations can do nothing to rescue themselves from this mad craze?

In the third story, where is the promised land for those suffering from AIDS? When these patients, who suffer pneumonia for the third or fourth time or wounds that can no longer be healed, cry out to God, "Oh! My Lord, deliver us from this sorrow," where can God lead them? When people like me, who care much about this modern tragedy, cry to God for their deliverance, all I can hear is my own hollow echo, "Will we ever see the light of your love again?"

It is always the case that it is just when we can no longer hear the voice of God that God's word in the Bible becomes so precious. It is when we can no longer read the Bible in the same way that all of a sudden we discover something new, something fundamental, that we had not seen before.

I have read the Exodus story so many times in the past because the story speaks to me. I identify with the cry of the Jewish people, because I, similarly, long for deliverance from the yoke of British rule. I never questioned that God interacted in history on behalf of the Jews when they needed God most. The powerful language of deliverance has sustained people in the Third World when we cannot see light at the end of the darkened tunnel. We have sung so many times:

> Will the night of bondage last forever?
> Will we ever sing the song of freedom?

Liberation theologians from South Korea and the Philippines have appropriated the Exodus story in their long and tortuous struggle against colonialism and dictatorship. Similarly, theologians in Latin America have found the Exodus story as the key to understanding liberation.

I first became aware that other people might look at the Exodus story differently when I listened some years ago to C. S. Song, a Presbyterian theologian from Taiwan. From the perspective of the tribal people in Taiwan, Song explained, the Exodus story is oppressive because the Canaanites were treated badly. Later, as I had the opportunities to visit the Maoris in New Zealand and the Aborigines in Australia, they shared similar insights. I had never read the story from the perspective of the Canaanites, and the experience was shocking to me.

Several months ago I read the book *Voices from the Margin: Interpreting the Bible in the Third World*, which contains six different perspectives on the Exodus story, from different parts of the world.[2] I became aware that American Indians also read the Exodus story from the side of the Canaanites, as Robert Allen Warrior writes:

> The obvious characters in the story for Native Americans to identify with are the Canaanites, the people who already lived in the promised land. As a member of the Osage Nation of American Indians who stands in solidarity with other tribal people around the world, I read the Exodus stories with Canaanite eyes. And, it is the Canaanite side of the story that has been overlooked by those seeking to articulate theologies of liberation. Especially ignored are those parts of the story that describe Yahweh's command to mercilessly annihilate the indigenous population.[3]

Ignoring the Canaanites of biblical times has led us to overlook the Canaanites of our time. The most difficult perspective for us is the Palestinian point of view. In *Justice, and Only Justice: A Palestinian Theology of Liberation*, Naim Stifan Ateek writes that before the creation of the state of Israel, the Hebrew Scriptures were considered to be an essential part of the Christian Bible, but after the establishment of the state, some have read the Hebrew Scriptures as a Zionist text. For Palestinian Christians, who have been part of the Christian family since the day of Jesus, the basic question is

"How can the Old Testament be the Word of God in the light of the Palestinian Christians' experience with its use to support Zionism?"[4]

To this question I have no answer. I only know that it was very difficult for me to meet face-to-face with Christians from Palestine and Iraq at the World Council of Churches seventh assembly, held at Canberra, when the Gulf War was going on. I guess Christians from the United States who were there felt even worse than I did. How could one listen to the Metropolitan from Iraq, who pleaded with us to stop the war in the name of the innocent children who had died, without feeling terrible remorse? What have we done to one another as human beings? I cried out, "God, have mercy on us."

It was on Yom Kippur, the day of repentance for the Jews, that I first heard a new Jewish perspective on the story. Marc H. Ellis, well known for his book *Toward a Jewish Theology of Liberation*,[5] came to Union Theological Seminary in New York on that very day in order to talk about justice for the Palestinians. He said Jews who have experienced the horrifying tragedy of the Holocaust must never use that painful memory as a tool to trample on the Palestinians. My heart said, "What courage, what wisdom."

Our story has come full circle. The promised land is a story first told by the Jews, and the Jews are now reinterpreting their story anew for us. But that voice is so small; the voices of prophets are always small. I ask myself, How can I make sense of all this? How can I read the story again? Where is the promised land now? It is as if my old faith is challenged, and the old religious system that once gave meaning to life is fundamentally called into question. Can I believe in a God who killed the Canaanites and who seems not to have listened to the cry of the Palestinians now for some forty years?

As always, when I am ready to throw this promised land story away because I can no longer deal with it, I hear something new. We must be extremely careful when we identify the promised land as our homeland. It is even more dangerous to identify it with somebody else's land. As I was looking for a new interpretation for the story, my help came, not from the theologians, but from a psychiatrist, Robert Jay Lifton. Lifton has spent his entire career studying the most tragic events of human history in the twentieth century: Hiroshima, the Holocaust, the Vietnam War, and the Chinese Cultural Revolution. He has written on the need to symbolize immortality when faced with suffering, senselessness, absurdity, and death.[6] I became suddenly aware that the promised land is one of the most powerful symbolizations of hope in the religious traditions of humankind. It is this capacity to hope that sustains us and moves us to action. It is in hope that we affirm that suffering and death are not the end.

To speak about hope in this world plagued with war, AIDS, and innocent deaths is not easy. We are facing calamities day after day. We can speak of a new promised land only if we are prepared to speak of a new Exodus. Here the wisdom of Second Isaiah is most helpful. Some fifty years after the Babylonian Exile, Second Isaiah spoke of a new Exodus and a new covenant with God. It was hope against all odds.

> Seek the Lord while he may be found,
> call upon him while he is near.
> . . . .
> For my thoughts are not your thoughts,
> nor are your ways my ways, says the Lord.
> . . . .
> For you shall go out in joy,
> and be led back in peace;
> the mountains and the hills before you
> shall burst into song
> and all the trees of the field shall clap their hands.
> . . . .
> and it shall be to the Lord for a memorial,
> for an everlasting sign that shall not be cut off.
>
> (Isa. 55)

Today, thirty months after the Tiananmen Square massacre, ten months after the Gulf War, and exactly ten years after the first incidence of AIDS in the United States, let us renew our hope in the promised land and together prepare ourselves for this new Exodus. Let us make a new covenant with one another and with God. Let us work together so that Moses' vision of a land filled with milk and honey will one day come true for every adult and every child on earth. It is precisely in this commitment to one another that the future of our hope lies. If we are to have a future at all, as Lifton says, it "exists within us now, here—at this moment and this place."[7]

NOTES

Prologue

1. From a poem written by a Beijing citizen on June 5, 1989, *Reflections* 3 (1989): 26. My own translation.

2. Jane Chui, "Mary in the Magnificat," *Diocesan Echo* 405 (1983): 3.

3. From "Declaration on Hunger Strike" by Beijing students, May 13, 1989. My own translation.

4. Ibid.

5. From the song "Blood-tainted Countenance," written by a Chinese soldier during a battle between China and Vietnam forces. It became very popular during the student demonstration in Beijing as the students went on a hunger strike. My own translation.

6. From the popular song "Descendants of the Dragon," written by a Taiwanese composer who later participated in the Tiananmen Square hunger strike. My own translation.

Introduction

1. Kwok Pui-lan, "Discovering the Bible in the Non-Biblical World," *Semeia* 47 (1989): 25-42.

2. I have used the term *Third World* as theologians in the Ecumenical Association of Third World Theologians (EATWOT) have understood it. Virginia Fabella writes: "For EATWOT, however, the term has a supra-geographic sense, describing a social condition characterized by poverty and oppression: massive poverty surrounding small pockets of affluence with an oppressed majority facing a powerful elite. The Third World is marked by economic, political, racial, gender and/or other forms of oppression; it is the underside of affluence and dominance." See *Beyond Bonding: A Third World Women's Theological Journey* (Manila: Ecumenical Association of Third World Theologians, 1993), 3. Aloysius Pieris also states: "The Third World is not merely the story of the South in relation to the North or of the East in relation to the West. It is something that happens wherever and whenever socio-economic dependence in terms of race, class, or sex generates political and cultural slavery, fermenting thereby a new peoplehood." See *An Asian Theology of Liberation* (Maryknoll, N.Y.: Orbis Books, 1988), 87.

3. See *Lift Every Voice: Constructing Christian Theologies from the Underside*, ed. Susan Brooks Thistlethwaite and Mary Porter Engel (San Francisco: Harper and Row, 1990), 270-82; *Voices from the Margin: Interpreting the Bible in*

the Third World, ed. R. S. Sugirtharajah (Maryknoll, N.Y.: Orbis Books, 1991), 299-315; and *The Bible and Liberation: Political and Social Hermeneutics*, rev. ed., ed. Norman K. Gottwald and Richard A. Horsley (Maryknoll, N.Y.: Orbis Books, 1993), 17-30.

4. Paul A. Cohen, *Discovering History in China: American Historical Writings on the Recent Chinese Past* (New York: Columbia University Press, 1984), 7.

5. "African Report," in *Third World Theologies: Commonalities and Divergences*, ed. K. C. Abraham (Maryknoll, N.Y.: Orbis Books, 1990), 41.

6. Women's Concerns Units, Christian Conference of Asia, ed., *Reading the Bible as Asian Women* (Singapore: Christian Conference of Asia, 1986).

7. Lee Oo Chung et al., eds., *Women of Courage: Asian Women Reading the Bible* (Seoul: Asian Women's Resource Center for Culture and Theology, 1992).

8. Hope S. Antone and Yong Tin Jin, eds., *Re-Living Our Faith Today: A Bible Study Resource Book* (Hong Kong: World Student Christian Federation, Asia-Pacific Region, 1992).

9. Only the Philippine paper has been published; see EATWOT Women in the Philippines and Asia, *Toward an Asian Principle of Interpretation: A Filipino Women's Experience* (Manila: Ecumenical Association of Third World Theologians, 1991).

10. For example, see Aruna Gnanadason, "Feminist Theology: An Indian Perspective," *In God's Image* (December 1988): 44-51; Sun Ai Lee Park, "Understanding the Bible from Women's Perspective," *Voices from the Third World* 10:2 (1987): 66-75.

11. Kwok Pui-lan, "Zhenfen funü de fuyin" (A Gospel that motivates women), in *Fengsheng de fuyin* (The fullness of the Gospel), ed. Joseph Kaung and Kwok Pui-lan (Hong Kong: Chung Chi College Theology Division, 1984), 92-108; and "The Feminist Hermeneutics of Elisabeth Schüssler Fiorenza: An Asian Feminist Response," *East Asia Journal of Theology* 3:2 (1985): 147-53.

12. Fernando F. Segovia posed this question to himself in his lecture at the Episcopal Divinity School, September 30, 1993.

13. This insight is shared by other students of Schwartz; see Tu Wei-ming, *Confucian Thought: Selfhood as Creative Transformation* (Albany, N.Y.: State University of New York Press, 1985), 16.

14. The notions of "multiple entries" and "different lines of growth" are taken from the editor's note to Gilles Deleuze and Félix Guattari, "What Is a Minor Literature?" *Mississippi Review* 22:3 (1983): 13-14.

15. Kwok Pui-lan, "Racism and Ethnocentrism in Feminist Biblical Interpretation," in *A Feminist Introduction*, vol. 1 of *Searching the Scriptures*, ed. Elisabeth Schüssler Fiorenza (New York: Crossroad, 1993), 101-16.

16. Edward W. Said, *Beginnings: Intention and Method* (New York: Basic Books, 1975), 8.

17. See Rey Chow, "Against the Lures of Diaspora: Minority Discourse, Chinese Women, and Intellectual Hegemony," in *Gender and Sexuality in Twentieth-Century Chinese Literature and Society*, ed. Tonglin Lu (Albany, N.Y.: State University of New York Press, 1993), 38.

1. Discovering the Bible in the Non-Biblical World

I am grateful to Kesaya Noda for editing the manuscript when it first appeared in *Semeia* and to the Asian Women Theologians, U.S. Group, for mutual support and encouragement.

1. T. C. Chao (Zhao Zichen), "The Articulate Word and the Problem of Communication," *International Review of Mission* 36 (1947): 482.

2. Michel Foucault, *Power/Knowledge: Selected Interviews and Other Writings, 1972-1977*, ed. Colin Gordon (New York: Pantheon Books, 1980), 131.

3. John R. Mott, *The Evangelization of the World in This Generation* (1900; reprint, New York: Arno Books, 1972), 17-18.

4. Jacques Lacan and the École Freudienne, *Feminine Sexuality*, ed. Juliet Mitchell and Jacqueline Rose; trans. Jacqueline Rose (New York: W. W. Norton, 1982), 74-85.

5. R. H. Graves, "How Shall the Native Church Be Stimulated to More Aggressive Christian Work?" in *Records of the General Conference of the Protestant Missionaries of China Held at Shanghai, May 10-24, 1877* (Shanghai: Presbyterian Mission Press, 1877), 339.

6. P. W. Pitcher, *A History of the Amoy Mission, China* (New York: Board of Publication of the Reformed Church in America, 1893), 47.

7. Hendrik Kraemer, *The Christian Message in a Non-Christian World*, 3d ed. (Grand Rapids, Mich.: Kregel, 1956), Table of Contents, 4.

8. Ibid., 102.

9. Hendrik Kraemer, "Continuity or Discontinuity," in *The Authority of the Faith* (New York: International Missionary Council, 1939), 1-21.

10. T. C. Chao, "Revelation," in *The Authority of the Faith*, 42.

11. Ibid., 43.

12. Bo Chenguang, "Zhongguo de jiuyue" (Chinese Old Testament) *Zhenli yu shengming* (Truth and life) 2 (1927): 240-44.

13. Xie Fuya, "Guanhu zhonghua Jidujiao shengjing de bianding wenti" (On the issues of editing the Chinese Christian Bible), in *Zhonghua Jidujiao shenxue lunji* (Chinese Christian theology anthology) (Hong Kong: Chinese Christian Book Giving Society, 1974), 39-40; and Hu Zanyun, "Liangbu jiuyu" (Two Old Testaments), ibid., 67-71.

14. Y. T. Wu (Wu Yaozhong), "The Orient Reconsiders Christianity," *Christian Century* 54 (1937): 836.

15. William R. Hutchison, "A Moral Equivalent for Imperialism: Americans and the Promotion of 'Christian Civilization,' 1880-1910," in *Missionary Ideologies in the Imperialist Era: 1880-1920*, ed. Torben Christensen and William R. Hutchison (Arthus, Denmark: Aros, 1982), 174.

16. Ng Lee-ming, "The Promise and Limitations of Chinese Protestant Theologians, 1920-1950," *Ching Feng* 21:4-22:1 (1978-1979): 178-79.

17. Wu, "The Orient Reconsiders Christianity," 837.

18. Ibid., 836.

19. Katie Geneva Cannon, "A Theological Analysis of Imperialistic Christianity," in *An Ocean with Many Shores: Asian Women Making Connections in Theology and Ministry*, ed. Nantawan Boonprasat Lewis (New York: Asian Women Theologians, Northeast U. S. Group, 1987), 25.

20. Kosuke Koyama, *Mount Fuji and Mount Sinai: A Critique of Idols* (Maryknoll, N.Y.: Orbis Books, 1984), 7-8.

21. Sharon Parks, *The Critical Years: The Young Adult Search for a Faith to Live By* (San Francisco: Harper and Row, 1986), 117.

22. Susan Brooks Thistlethwaite, "Every Two Minutes: Battered Women and Feminist Interpretation," in *Feminist Interpretation of the Bible*, ed. Letty Russell (Philadelphia: Westminster, 1985), 98.

23. Parks, *The Critical Years*, 113.

24. C. S. Song, *Theology from the Womb of Asia* (Maryknoll, N.Y.: Orbis Books, 1986), 16.

25. C. S. Song, *The Tears of Lady Meng* (Geneva: World Council of Churches, 1981).

26. C. S. Song, *Tell Us Our Names: Story Theology from an Asian Perspective* (Maryknoll, N.Y.: Orbis Books, 1984), x.

27. Maen Pongudom, "Creation of Man: Theological Reflections Based on Northern Thai Folktales," *East Asia Journal of Theology* 3:2 (1985): 227.

28. Archie C. C. Lee, "The David-Bathsheba Story and the Parable of Nathan," in *Voices from the Margin*, 202.

29. Padma Gallup, "Doing Theology—An Asian Feminist Perspective," *Commission on Theological Concerns Bulletin, Christian Conference of Asia* 4 (1983): 22.

30. Kwok Pui-lan, "God Weeps with Our Pain," *East Asia Journal of Theology* 2:2 (1984): 228-32.

31. Kwok Pui-lan, "A Chinese Perspective," in *Theology by the People: Reflections on Doing Theology in Community*, ed. Samuel Amirtham and John S. Pobee (Geneva: World Council of Churches, 1986), 78-83.

32. Nantawan Boonprasat Lewis, "Asian Women Theology: A Historical and Theological Analysis," *East Asia Journal of Theology* 4:2 (1986): 21.

33. Kim Yong Bock, "Messiah and Minjung: Discerning Messianic Politics over against Political Messianism," in *Minjung Theology: People as the Subjects of History*, ed. Kim Yong Bock (Singapore: Commission on Theological Concerns, Christian Conference of Asia, 1981), 186.

34. Kim Yong Bock, "Minjung Social Biography and Theology," *Ching Feng* 28:4 (1985): 224.

35. Cyris H. S. Moon, *A Korean Minjung Theology: An Old Testament Perspective* (Maryknoll, N.Y.: Orbis Books, 1985).

36. Ahn Byung Mu, "Jesus and the Minjung in the Gospel of Mark," in *Minjung Theology*, 138-39.

37. Suh Nam Dong, "Historical References for a Theology of Minjung," in *Minjung Theology*, 160.

38. Ibid., 159.

39. Sung-hee Lee, "Women's Liberation Theology as the Foundation for Asian Theology," *East Asia Journal of Theology* 4:2 (1986): 2-13.

40. Robert Detweiler, "Introduction," *Semeia* 23 (1982): 1.

41. See Chad Hansen, "Chinese Ideographs and Western Ideas," *Journal of Asian Studies* 52 (1993): 373-99.

42. Jonathan Culler, *On Deconstruction: Theory and Criticism after Structuralism* (Ithaca, N.Y.: Cornell University Press, 1982), 128.

43. Robert Detweiler, "What Is a Sacred Text?" *Semeia* 31 (1985): 217.

44. Carol P. Christ, "Spiritual Quest and Women's Experience," in *Womanspirit Rising: A Feminist Reader in Religion*, ed. Carol P. Christ and Judith Plaskow (San Francisco: Harper and Row, 1979), 229-30.

45. Ibid., 231.

46. Rosemary Radford Ruether, *Womanguides: Reading toward a Feminist Theology* (Boston: Beacon, 1985).

47. Elisabeth Schüssler Fiorenza, *In Memory of Her: A Feminist Theological Reconstruction of Christian Origins* (New York: Crossroad, 1983).

48. Carol P. Christ, *Diving Deep and Surfacing: Women Writers on Spiritual Quest* (Boston: Beacon, 1980).

49. Katie Geneva Cannon, *Black Womanist Ethics* (Atlanta: Scholars Press, 1988); Delores S. Williams, *Sisters in the Wilderness: The Challenge of Womanist Theology* (Maryknoll, N.Y.: Orbis Books, 1993).

50. Rosemary Radford Ruether, "Feminist Interpretation: A Method of Correlation," in *Feminist Interpretation of the Bible*, 117.

51. Elisabeth Schüssler Fiorenza, "The Will to Choose or to Reject: Continuing Our Critical Work," in *Feminist Interpretation of the Bible*, 131.

2. The Bible, the Critic, and the Theologian

1. Wilfred Cantwell Smith, "The Study of Religion and the Study of the Bible," in *Rethinking Scripture: Essays from a Comparative Perspective*, ed. Miriam Levering (Albany, N.Y.: State University of New York Press, 1989), 22.

2. Wilfred Cantwell Smith, *What Is Scripture? A Comparative Approach* (Minneapolis: Fortress, 1993), 6.

3. For example, see Levering, *Rethinking Scripture*; Smith, *What Is Scripture?*; Frederick M. Denny and Rodney L. Taylor, eds., *The Holy Book in Comparative Perspective* (Columbia, S.C.: University of South Carolina Press, 1985); Harold Coward, *Sacred Word and Sacred Text: Scripture in World Religions* (Maryknoll, N.Y.: Orbis Books, 1988); Muslim-Christian Research Group, *The Challenge of the Scriptures: The Bible and the Qur'an* (Maryknoll, N.Y.: Orbis Books, 1989).

4. William A. Graham, *Beyond the Written Word: Oral Aspects of Scripture in the History of Religion* (Cambridge: Cambridge University Press, 1987), 2-5.

5. Miriam Levering, "Introduction," in *Rethinking Scripture*, 2; Smith, *What Is Scripture?*, 17-18; and Graham, *Beyond the Written Word*, 170.

6. Rodney L. Taylor, "Confucianism: Scripture and the Sage," in *The Holy Book in Comparative Perspective*, 181-203; see also Smith, *What Is Scripture?*, 176-83.

7. See Reginald A. Ray, "Buddhism: Sacred Text Written and Realized," in *The Holy Book in Comparative Perspective*, 148-80; and Laurence G. Thompson, "Taoism: Classic and Canon," ibid., 204-23.

8. Tu, *Confucian Thought*, 55.

9. James Barr, *Fundamentalism* (Philadelphia: Westminster, 1977), 11-39.

10. R. S. Sugirtharajah, "Inter-faith Hermeneutics: An Example and Some Implications," in *Voices from the Margin*, 353.

11. Asian Theological Conference III Participants, "The Search for a Liberation Spirituality in Asia," in *Asian Christian Spirituality: Reclaiming Traditions*, ed. Virginia Fabella, Peter K. H. Lee, and David Kwang-sun Suh (Maryknoll, N.Y.: Orbis Books, 1992), 148.

12. Pieris, *An Asian Theology of Liberation*, 69.

13. Aruna Gnanadason, "Women and Spirituality in Asia," *In God's Image* (December 1989): 15-18; and "A Spirituality that Sustains Us in Our Struggles," *International Review of Mission* 80 (1991): 29-41.

14. C. S. Song, *Tell Us Our Names*; idem, *Jesus, the Crucified People* (New York: Crossroad, 1990); idem, *Jesus and the Reign of God* (Minneapolis: Fortress, 1993).

15. Chung Hyun Kyung, *Struggle to Be the Sun Again: Introducing Asian Women's Theology* (Maryknoll, N.Y.: Orbis Books, 1990).

16. See, for example, Elizabeth V. Spelman, *Inessential Women: Problems of Exclusion in Feminist Thought* (Boston: Beacon, 1988); Marianne Hirsch and Evelyn Fox Keller, eds., *Conflicts in Feminism* (New York: Routledge, 1990); Michèle Barrett and Anne Phillips, eds., *Destabilizing Theory: Contemporary Feminist Debates* (Stanford: Stanford University Press, 1992).

17. Chung, *Struggle to Be the Sun Again*, 23-24.

18. Williams, *Sisters in the Wilderness*.

19. Ada María Isasi-Díaz, *En la Lucha/In the Struggle: An Hispanic Women's Theology* (Minneapolis: Fortress, 1993).

20. Sharon D. Welch, "Sporting Power: American Feminism, French Feminisms, and an Ethic of Conflict," in *Transfigurations: Theology and the French Feminists*, ed. C. W. Maggie Kim, Susan M. St. Ville, and Susan M. Simonaitis (Minneapolis: Fortress, 1993), 176.

21. See the different points of view of Sharon D. Welch, "Sporting Power," and Ellen T. Armour, "Questioning 'Woman' in Feminist/Womanist Theology: Iragaray, Ruether, and Daly," in *Transfigurations*, 171-98 and 143-69. See also Teresa de Lauretis, "Upping the Anti [sic] in Feminist Theory," in *Conflicts in Feminism*, 255-70.

22. Linda Alcoff, "Cultural Feminism versus Post-Structuralism: The Identity Crisis in Feminist Theory," *Signs* 13 (1988): 433.

23. See Patricia Hill Collins, *Black Feminist Thought: Knowledge, Consciousness, and the Politics of Empowerment* (London: HarperCollins Academic, 1990), 233-35.

24. See Paulos Gregorios, "The Hermeneutical Discussion in India Today," *Indian Journal of Theology* 31:3-4 (1982): 153-55.

25. R. S. Sugirtharajah, "The Bible and Its Asian Readers," *Biblical Interpretation* 1:1 (1993): 54-66.

26. See Mae Gwendolyn Henderson, "Speaking in Tongues: Dialogics, Dialectics, and the Black Woman Writer's Literary Tradition," in *Reading Black,*

Reading Feminist: A Critical Anthology, ed. Henry Louis Gates, Jr. (New York: Meridian Books, 1990), 117.

27. R. S. Sugirtharajah, "'What Do Men Say Remains of Me?': Current Jesus Research and Third World Christologies," *Asia Journal of Theology* 5:2 (1991): 336.

28. Barbara Christian, *Black Feminist Criticism: Perspectives on Black Women Writers* (New York: Pergamon, 1985); Henry Louis Gates, Jr., *The Signifying Monkey: A Theory of African-American Literary Criticism* (New York: Oxford University Press, 1988).

29. Ashis Nandy, *The Intimate Enemy: Loss and Recovery of Self under Colonialism* (Delhi: Oxford University Press, 1983).

30. Edward W. Said, *Orientalism* (New York: Pantheon Books, 1978); Gayatri Chakravorty Spivak, *Outside in the Teaching Machine* (New York: Routledge, 1993).

31. James H. Cone, *A Black Theology of Liberation,* 2d ed. (Maryknoll, N.Y.: Orbis Books, 1990), 29-32.

32. See Itumeleng J. Mosala, *Biblical Hermeneutics and Black Theology in South Africa* (Grand Rapids, Mich.: William B. Eerdmans, 1989), 13-42.

33. C. S. Song, "From Israel to Asia: A Theological Leap," *Ecumenical Review* 28 (1976): 252-65.

34. Kosuke Koyama, *No Handle on the Cross* (Maryknoll, N.Y.: Orbis Books, 1977) and *Three Mile an Hour God* (Maryknoll, N.Y.: Orbis Books, 1980).

35. Williams, *Sisters in the Wilderness,* 146.

36. Ibid., 146-47.

37. Mosala, *Biblical Hermeneutics and Black Theology,* 18.

38. Ibid., 193.

39. Ibid., 20.

40. Gnanadason, "Feminist Theology: An Indian Perspective," 47.

41. Chung, *Struggle to Be the Sun Again,* 113.

42. Cornel West, *Keeping Faith: Philosophy and Race in America* (New York: Routledge, 1993), 89.

43. Nandy, *The Intimate Enemy,* 11.

44. West, *Keeping Faith,* 89.

3. Toward a Dialogical Model of Interpretation

1. I am thinking of the works of Ahn Byung Mu, Chung Hyun Kyung, David Kwang-sun Suh, and Suh Nam Dong of Korea; Hisako Kinukawa of Japan; Aloysius Pieris and R. S. Sugirtharajah of Sri Lanka; George M. Soares-Prabhu, Stanley J. Samartha, and Paulos Gregorios of India; C. S. Song of Taiwan; and Archie Lee and myself from Hong Kong.

2. See, for example, Norman R. Petersen, *Literary Criticism for New Testament Critics* (Philadelphia: Fortress, 1978); Lynn M. Poland, *Literary Criticism and Biblical Hermeneutics: A Critique of Formalist Approaches* (Chico, Calif.: Scholars Press, 1985).

3. Jacques Derrida, *Of Grammatology,* trans. Gayatri Chakravorty Spivak (Baltimore: Johns Hopkins University Press, 1974), 80.

4. Ibid., 79.

5. S. Robert Ramsey, *The Languages of China* (Princeton: Princeton University Press, 1987), 49-57.

6. See Julia Kristeva, *Language: The Unknown, an Initiation into Linguistics*, trans. Anne M. Menke (New York: Columbia University Press, 1989), 78.

7. See Yen Ren Chao, *Aspects of Chinese Sociolinguistics* (Stanford: Stanford University Press, 1976), 25, 72-83.

8. Ramsey, *The Languages of China*, 99.

9. Chao, *Aspects of Chinese Sociolinguistics*, 263.

10. Ramsey, *The Languages of China*, 137.

11. M. M. Bakhtin, *The Dialogic Imagination: Four Essays*, ed. Michael Holquist, trans. Caryl Emerson and Michael Holquist (Austin: University of Texas Press, 1981), 293.

12. See Cathy Silber, "From Daughter to Daughter-in-law in the Women's Script in Southern Hunan," in *Engendering China: Women, Culture, and the State*, ed. Christina K. Gilmartin, Gail Hershatter, Lisa Rofel, and Tyrene White (Cambridge, Mass.: Harvard University Press, 1994), 47-68.

13. Chang Tung-sun (Zhang Dongsun), "A Chinese Philosopher's Theory of Knowledge," *Yenching Journal of Social Studies* 1:2 (1939): 165.

14. Ibid., 167.

15. Ibid., 169.

16. Chen Chi-yun (Chen Qiyun), "Chinese Language and Truth—A Critique of Chad Hansen's Analysis," *Chinese Culture Quarterly* 31:2 (1990): 70.

17. Benjamin I. Schwartz, *The World of Thought in Ancient China* (Cambridge, Mass.: Belknap Press, 1985), 89.

18. Ibid., 94.

19. Chad Hansen, "Chinese Language, Chinese Philosophy, and 'Truth,'" *Journal of Asian Studies* 44 (1985): 494. For a critique of Hansen, see Chen Chi-yun, "Chinese Language and Truth."

20. See Hansen, "Chinese Language," 495.

21. Schwartz, *The World of Thought*, 93.

22. Tu, *Confucian Thought*, 57.

23. Bakhtin, *The Dialogic Imagination*, 262-63.

24. Ibid., 292.

25. Ken Hirschkop and David Shepherd, eds., *Bakhtin and Cultural Theory* (Manchester: Manchester University Press, 1989), 6.

26. Evelyn Brooks Higginbotham, *Righteous Discontent: The Women's Movement in the Black Baptist Church, 1880-1920* (Cambridge, Mass.: Harvard University Press, 1993), 16.

27. See Mary McClintock Fulkerson, *Changing the Subject: Women's Discourses and Feminist Theology* (Minneapolis: Fortress, 1994).

28. Wendy Doniger O'Flaherty, "The Uses and Misuses of Other Peoples' Myths," *Journal of the American Academy of Religion* 54 (1986): 224.

29. See the discussion in David Carroll, "Narrative, Heterogeneity and the Question of the Political: Bakhtin and Lyotard," in *The Aims of Representation: Subject/Text/History*, ed. Murray Krieger (Stanford: Stanford University Press, 1993), 77.

30. Sheila Briggs, "The Politics of Identity and the Politics of Interpretation," *Union Seminary Quarterly Review* 43 (1989): 163-80.

31. bell hooks, *Feminist Theory: From Margin to Center* (Boston: South End Press, 1984); Deborah K. King, "Multiple Jeopardy, Multiple Consciousness: The Context of a Black Feminist Ideology," *Signs* 14 (1988): 42-72; Rose M. Brewer, "Theorizing Race, Class, and Gender: The New Scholarship of Black Feminist Intellectuals and Black Women's Labor," in *Theorizing Black Feminisms: The Visionary Pragmatism of Black Women*, ed. Stanlie M. James and Abena P. A. Busia (New York: Routledge, 1993), 13-30.

32. Evelyn Brooks Higginbotham, "African-American Women's History and the Metalanguage of Race," *Signs* 17 (1992): 251-74.

33. Audre Lorde, "Eye to Eye," in *Sister Outsider* (Trumansburg, N.Y.: Crossing Press, 1984), 147.

34. Itumeleng J. Mosala, "The Implications of the Text of Esther for African Women's Struggle for Liberation in South Africa," *Semeia* 59 (1992): 129-37.

35. Pieris, *An Asian Theology of Liberation*, xv.

36. Ibid., 15-23, 120-26.

37. To understand how people from other cultures talk about postmodernism, see bell hooks, "Postmodern Blackness," in *Yearning: Race, Gender, and Cultural Politics* (Boston: South End Press, 1990), 23-31; Cornel West, "The Postmodern Crisis of Black Intellectuals," in *Prophetic Thought in Postmodern Times*, vol. 1 of *Beyond Eurocentrism and Multiculturalism* (Monroe, Maine: Common Courage Press, 1993), 87-118; Philip Brian Harper, *Framing the Margins: The Social Logic of Postmodern Culture* (New York: Oxford University Press, 1994).

38. See Bill Ashcroft, Gareth Griffiths, and Helen Tiffin, *The Empire Writes Back: Theory and Practice in Post-Colonial Literature* (London: Routledge, 1989), 162-63, 172-73.

39. See Fredric Jameson, *The Political Unconscious: Narrative as a Socially Symbolic Act* (Ithaca, N.Y.: Cornell University Press, 1981).

40. Elisabeth Schüssler Fiorenza, *But She Said: Feminist Practices of Biblical Interpretation* (Boston: Beacon, 1992), 151.

41. Elisabeth Schüssler Fiorenza, *Bread Not Stone: The Challenge of Feminist Biblical Interpretation* (Boston: Beacon, 1984), 25-28.

42. See the discussion in Claudia V. Camp, "Feminist Theological Hermeneutics: Canon and Christian Identity," in *A Feminist Introduction*, vol. 1 of *Searching the Scriptures*, 154-71. Camp agrees more with the models of Schüssler Fiorenza and McFague than does this author.

43. Schüssler Fiorenza, *But She Said*, 149.

44. Ibid., 80-101.

45. Karen Baker-Fletcher, "Anna Julia Cooper and Sojourner Truth: Two Nineteenth-Century Black Feminist Interpreters of Scripture," in *A Feminist Introduction*, vol. 1 of *Searching the Scriptures*, 41-51; and Cheryl Townsend Gilkes, "'Mother to the Motherless, Father to the Fatherless': Power, Gender, and Community in an Afrocentric Biblical Tradition," *Semeia* 47 (1989): 57-85.

46. Schüssler Fiorenza, *In Memory of Her*, 140-51.

47. Sallie McFague, *Metaphorical Theology: Models of God in Religious Language* (Philadelphia: Fortress, 1982), 54-66.

48. David Tracy, *The Analogical Imagination: Christian Theology and the Culture of Pluralism* (New York: Crossroad, 1981), 108.

49. McFague, *Metaphorical Theology*, 63.

50. Ibid., 62.

51. See the discussion in Krister Stendahl, "The Bible as a Classic and the Bible as Holy Scripture," *Journal of Biblical Literature* 103 (1984): 3-10; and Smith, *What Is Scripture?*, 176-95.

52. See George M. Soares-Prabhu, "From Alienation to Inculturation: Some Reflections on Doing Theology in India Today," in *Bread and Breath: Essays in Honor of Samuel Ryan, S.J.*, ed. T. K. John (Anand, Gujarat: Gujarat Sahitya Prakash, 1991), 55-99.

53. The metaphor of "talking book" is taken from Gates, *The Signifying Monkey*, 127-69.

54. Ibid.

55. Gilkes, "Mother to the Motherless," 57.

56. Renita J. Weems, "Reading *Her Way* through the Struggle: African American Women and the Bible," in *Stony the Road We Trod: African American Biblical Interpretation*, ed. Cain Hope Felder (Minneapolis: Fortress, 1991), 76.

57. M. M. Bakhtin (V. N. Voloshinov, pseudo.), *Marxism and the Philosophy of Language*, trans. L. Matejka and I. R. Titunik (New York: Seminar Press, 1973), 115.

4. Hearing and Talking: Oral Hermeneutics of Asian Women

1. Teresa Okure, "Feminist Interpretations in Africa," in *A Feminist Introduction*, vol. 1 of *Searching the Scriptures*, 83.

2. Weems, "Reading *Her Way*," 66; see also Vincent L. Wimbush, "Historical/Cultural Criticism as Liberation: A Proposal for an African American Biblical Hermeneutic," *Semeia* 47 (1989): 45.

3. Cornel West, *Prophetic Fragments* (Grand Rapids, Mich.: William B. Eerdmans, 1988), 5.

4. Carlos Mesters, "The Use of the Bible in Christian Communities of the Common People," in *The Challenge of Basic Christian Communities*, ed. Sergio Torres and John Eagleson (Maryknoll, N.Y.: Orbis Books, 1981), 197-210.

5. Werner H. Kelber, *The Oral and the Written Gospel: The Hermeneutics of Speaking and Writing in the Synoptic Tradition, Mark, Paul, and Q* (Philadelphia: Fortress, 1983), 2.

6. Graham, *Beyond the Written Word*, 67-77; and Thomas B. Coburn, "'Scripture' in India: Towards a Typology of the Word in Hindu Life," in *Rethinking Scripture*, 102-28.

7. Stanley J. Samartha, "The Cross and the Rainbow: Christ in a Multireligious Culture," in *The Myth of Christian Uniqueness: Toward a Pluralistic Theology of Religions*, ed. John Hick and Paul F. Knitter (Maryknoll, N.Y.: Orbis Books, 1987), 78.

8. Arthur Waley, *The Analects of Confucius* (London: George Allen and Unwin, 1938), 21-26.

9. D. C. Lau, *Lao Tzu: Tao Te Ching* (New York: Penguin Books, 1963), 12; Ellen M. Chen, *The Tao Te Ching: A New Translation with Commentary* (New York: Paragon House, 1989), 19.

10. Miriam Levering, "Scripture and Its Reception: A Buddhist Case," in *Rethinking Scripture*, 61.

11. Joseph Needham, *Science and Civilization in China* (Cambridge: Cambridge University Press, 1956), 2:134.

12. Rita M. Gross, *Buddhism after Patriarchy: A Feminist History, Analysis, and Reconstruction of Buddhism* (Albany, N.Y.: State University of New York Press, 1993), 32.

13. Jack Goody, *The Interface between the Written and the Oral* (Cambridge: Cambridge University Press, 1987), 121-22.

14. Coward, *Sacred Word and Sacred Text*, 120.

15. Ibid., 118; Goody, *The Interface between the Written and the Oral*, 119.

16. Graham, *Beyond the Written Word*, 88-90; Frederick M. Denny, "Islam: Qur'an and Hadith," in *The Holy Book in Comparative Perspective*, 96-97.

17. Female literacy rates in China after the sixteenth century have been rising. See Susan Mann, "Learned Women in the Eighteenth Century," in *Engendering China*, 27-46.

18. William Barrett, ed., *Zen Buddhism: Selected Writings of D. T. Suzuki* (Garden City, N.Y.: Doubleday Anchor Books, 1956), 9.

19. Susan Naquin, *Millenarian Rebellion in China: The Eight Trigrams Uprising of 1813* (New Haven: Yale University Press, 1976), 41.

20. Levering, "Scripture and Its Reception," 68.

21. Lamin Sanneh, *Translating the Message: The Missionary Impact on Culture* (Maryknoll, N.Y.: Orbis Books, 1990), 213.

22. Ibid., 233-34.

23. Ibid., 101-2.

24. Wang Weifan, "The Bible in Chinese," *China Theological Review* 8 (1993): 100-23.

25. For a detailed study of the Chinese case, see Kwok Pui-lan, *Chinese Women and Christianity, 1860-1927* (Atlanta: Scholars Press, 1992), 65-100.

26. I benefit from the analysis of Evelyn Brooks Higginbotham of the black Baptist church (see *Righteous Discontent*, 14-15).

27. Kelber, *The Oral and the Written Gospel*, 18.

28. Walter J. Ong, "Text as Interpretation: Mark and After," *Semeia* 39 (1987): 11.

29. Joanna Dewey, "Mark as Interwoven Tapestry: Forecasts and Echoes for a Listening Audience," *Catholic Biblical Quarterly* 53 (1991): 235.

30. Charles H. Lohr, "Oral Techniques in the Gospel of Matthew," *Catholic Biblical Quarterly* 23 (1961): 403-35.

31. Joanna Dewey, "From Storytelling to the Written Text: The Loss of Early Christian Women's Voices," Unpublished paper.

32. Antoinette Clark Wire, "Gender Roles in a Scribal Community," in *Social History of the Matthean Community*, ed. David L. Balch (Minneapolis: Fortress, 1991), 121.

33. Walter J. Ong, *The Presence of the Word: Some Prolegomena for Cultural and Religious History* (New Haven: Yale University Press, 1967).

34. Schüssler Fiorenza, *Bread Not Stone*, 27.

35. Mary McClintock Fulkerson observes that many of the proponents of reader-response criticism rely upon the objective text to control meaning, see *Changing the Subject*, 135.

36. See Sandra M. Schneiders, *The Revelatory Text: Interpreting the New Testament as Sacred Scripture* (San Francisco: Harper SanFrancisco, 1991), 97-179.

37. Ong, *The Presence of the Word*, 24-26.

38. See the discussion in Deborah Tannen, "The Oral/Literate Continuum in Discourse," in *Spoken and Written Language: Exploring Orality and Literacy*, ed. Deborah Tannen (Norwood, N.J.: Ablex, 1982), 1-3.

39. Ong, *The Presence of the Word*, 25-29.

40. David R. Olson, "From Utterance to Text: The Bias of Language in Speech and Writing," *Harvard Educational Review* 47:3 (1977): 277.

41. Goody, *The Interface between the Written and the Oral*, 164.

42. See Susan Lochrie Graham, "Silent Voices: Women in the Gospel of Mark," *Semeia* 54 (1991): 145-58. Graham suggests we listen to the language of the body, figured by touch, instead of the language of the mind (speech and hearing).

43. Phyllis Trible, *Texts of Terror: Literary-Feminist Readings of Biblical Narratives* (Philadelphia: Fortress, 1984).

44. Lee Oo Chung, Sylvia Jenkin, and Mizuho Matsuda, "Introduction," in *Reading the Bible as Asian Women*, 1.

45. Crescy John, Susan, Sun Ai Lee Park, Pearl Drego, Pauline, Mary Lobo, and Margaret Shanti, "The Exodus Story," *In God's Image* (September 1988): 43.

46. Ibid., 45.

47. Pearl Drego, "Annunciation," *In God's Image* (December 1989): 11-14.

48. Marianne Katoppo, *Compassionate and Free: An Asian Woman's Theology* (Geneva: World Council of Churches, 1979), 22-24; Chung, *Struggle to Be the Sun Again*, 74-84; Rosemary Radford Ruether, *Mary—The Feminine Face of the Church* (London: SCM, 1979), 27.

49. Drego, "Annunciation," 12.

50. Ibid.

51. A. K. Ramanujan, "Tell It to the Walls: On Folktales in Indian Culture," in *India Briefing, 1992*, ed. L. A. Gordon and P. Oldenburg (Boulder: Westview Press, 1992), 167-68.

52. For example, "The Samaritan Woman," *In God's Image* (September 1988): 40-42; "The Exodus Story," ibid., 43-48; and "Waiting to Be Recognized," ibid., 49-50.

53. Elsa Tamez, "The Woman Who Complicated the History of Salvation," in *New Eyes for Reading: Biblical and Theological Reflections by Women from the Third World*, ed. John S. Pobee and Bärbel von Wartenberg-Potter (Oak Parks, Ill.: Meyer Stone Books, 1987), 5-17; and Williams, *Sisters in the Wilderness*, 15-33.

54. I find Bakhtin's expression "internal dialogization" very illuminating, though he refers more specifically to his philosophical understanding of language. See Bakhtin, *The Dialogic Imagination*, 280-84.

55. The idea of "voice into existence" is from Henry Louis Gates, Jr., "Talkin' that Talk," in *"Race," Writing, and Difference*, ed. Henry Louis Gates, Jr. (Chicago: University of Chicago Press, 1985), 403.

56. See Bakhtin, *The Dialogic Imagination*, 342-47. The fact that I use Bakhtin's work on the novel in the context of biblical hermeneutics illustrates the possibility of further dialogic interaction with Bakhtin's work.

57. A report of the visit is found in *In God's Image* 10:3 (Autumn 1991).

5. Speaking Many Tongues: Issues in Multifaith Hermeneutics

1. Chung Hyun Kyung, "Come, Holy Spirit—Renew the Whole Creation," in *Signs of the Spirit: Official Report, Seventh Assembly*, ed. Michael Kinnamon (Geneva: World Council of Churches, 1991), 37-47.

2. Jeffrey Gros, "Christian Confession in a Pluralistic World," *Christian Century* 108:20 (June 26-July 3, 1991): 645.

3. See the discussion on indigenization in *Jindai huaren shenxue wenxian* (A source book of modern Chinese theology), ed. Lam Wing-hung (Hong Kong: China Graduate School of Theology, 1986), 623-700.

4. For example, M. M. Thomas, *The Acknowledged Christ of the Indian Renaissance* (London: SCM, 1969).

5. Stanley J. Samartha, *Courage for Dialogue: Ecumenical Issues in Inter-Religious Relationships* (Geneva: World Council of Churches, 1981), 13.

6. Wesley Ariarajah, *The Bible and People of Other Faiths* (Maryknoll, N.Y.: Orbis Books, 1989), 3.

7. Ibid., 6-12, 36-38.

8. Ibid., 13-18.

9. Ibid., 39-47.

10. See, for example, D. Preman Niles, "Examples of Contextualization in the Old Testament," *South East Asia Journal of Theology* 21:2-22:1 (1980-1981): 19-33; Saphir P. Athyal, "Toward an Asian Christian Theology," in *Asian Christian Theology: Emerging Themes*, ed. Douglas J. Elwood (Philadelphia: Westminster, 1980), 69-71.

11. E. C. John, "Israel and Inculturation: An Appraisal," *Jeevadhara* 14 (1984): 87-94.

12. George Koonthanam, "The Prophets and the Nations," *Jeevadhara* 14 (1984): 133.

13. C. S. Song, "Living Theology: Birth and Rebirth," in *Doing Theology with Asian Resources: Ten Years in the Formation of Living Theology in Asia*, ed. John C. England and Archie C. C. Lee (Hong Kong: Program for Theology and Cultures in Asia, 1993), 7-11.

14. Carol P. Christ, "On Not Blaming Jews for the Death of the Goddess," in *Laughter of Aphrodite: Reflection on a Journey to the Goddess* (San Francisco: Harper and Row, 1987), 83-92.

15. Judith Plaskow, *Standing Again at Sinai: Judaism from a Feminist Perspective* (San Francisco: Harper and Row, 1990), 147-54.

16. Sugirtharajah, "Inter-faith Hermeneutics," 354.

17. Ibid., 356.

18. Ibid., 356-59.

19. Khiok-khng Yeo, "The Rhetorical Hermeneutic of 1 Corinthians 8 and Chinese Ancestor worship," *Biblical Interpretation* 2:3 (1994): 294-311.

20. Archie C. C. Lee, "Theological Reading of Chinese Creation Stories of P'an Ku and Nu Kua," in *Doing Theology with Asian Resources*, 230-37; and "The Chinese Creation Myth of Nu Kua and the Biblical Narrative in Genesis 1-11," *Biblical Interpretation* 2:3 (1994):312-24. I have rendered Nu Kua as Nüwa, following the Chinese *pinyin* system of romanization.

21. Lee, "The Chinese Creation Myth of Nu Kua," 317-22.

22. Lee, "Theological Reading of Chinese Creation Stories," 236.

23. George M. Soares-Prabhu, "Two Mission Commands: An Interpretation of Matthew 28:16-20 in the Light of a Buddhist Text," *Biblical Interpretation* 2:3 (1994): 281.

24. Ibid., 282.

25. Archie C. C. Lee, "Biblical Interpretation in Asian Perspectives," *Asia Journal of Theology* 7:1 (1993): 38.

26. Robert Ellsberg, ed., *Gandhi on Christianity* (Maryknoll, N.Y.: Orbis Books, 1991), 27.

27. Ibid., 28-29.

28. Ibid., 29.

29. Seiichi Yagi, "'I' in the Words of Jesus," in *The Myth of Christian Uniqueness*, 117-34.

30. Published as occasional papers of the Association for Theological Education in South East Asia. Available from ATESEA, 324 Onan Road, Singapore 1542, Republic of Singapore.

31. Lee, "Biblical Interpretative from Asian Perspectives," 36.

32. D. Preman Niles, "The Word of God and the People of Asia," in *Understanding the Word: Essays in Honor of Bernhard W. Anderson*, ed. James T. Butler, Edgar W. Conrad, and Ben C. Ollenburger (Sheffield: Journal for the Study of the Old Testament, 1985), 283.

33. C. S. Song, *Jesus, the Crucified People*, 12-14.

34. C. S. Song, "Programme for Theology and Christian [Cultures] in Asia—A Fresh Beginning for Christian Theology," in *Doing Theology with Cultures of Asia*, ed. Yeow Choo Lak (Singapore: ATESEA, 1988), 6.

35. Yuko Yuasa, "Sexuality of Sacrifice: A Spirituality of Noh Drama," in *Doing Theology with Asian Resources*, 112-25; see also "The Spirit Moves through the Spirits in Noh Drama: A Study of the Man-Woman Relationship," in *Doing Theology with the Spirit's Movement in Asia*, ed. John C. England and Alan J. Torrance (Singapore: ATESEA, 1991), 44-61.

36. Yuasa, "Sexuality of Sacrifice," 124-25.

37. Levi V. Oracion, "Theological Reflections on Indarapatra and S. Sulayman," *East Asia Journal of Theology* 3:2 (1985): 213-21.

38. Niles, "The Word of God and the People of Asia," 303.

39. There has been some discussion of various methods of interpretation of Asian scriptures, but not much on applying those insights to the study of the Bible. See, for example, D. S. Amalorpavadass, ed., *Research Seminar on Non-Biblical Scriptures* (Bangalore: National Biblical, Catechetical, and Liturgical Center, 1974), and the special issue on biblical hermeneutics in *Indian Journal of Theology* 31:3-4 (1982).

40. Suh Nam Dong, "Cultural Theology, Political Theology and Minjung Theology," *Commission on Theological Concerns Bulletin, Christian Conference in Asia* 5:3-6:1 (1984-1985): 14.

41. A recent example is John B. Henderson's, *Scripture, Canon, and Commentary: A Comparison of Confucian and Western Exegesis* (Princeton: Princeton University Press, 1991).

42. Gregorios, "The Hermeneutical Discussion in India Today," 153.

43. Stanley J. Samartha, *One Christ—Many Religions: Toward a Revised Christology* (Maryknoll: N.Y.: Orbis Books, 1991), 70-71.

44. Yü Ying-shih, *Lishi yu sixiang* (History and thought) (Taibei: Linjing Publisher, 1976), 250-51.

45. D. Preman Niles, "Story and Theology—A Proposal," *East Asia Journal of Theology* 3:1 (1985): 125.

46. Song, *Tell Us Our Names*, 40.

47. Suh, "Cultural Theology, Political Theology and Minjung Theology," 12-15.

48. Francis D'Sa, "The Challenge of the Indian Christian Tradition," as quoted in Niles, "The Word of God and the People of Asia," 302-3.

49. Choi Man Ja, "Feminine Images of God in Korean Traditional Religion," in *Frontiers in Asian Christian Theology: Emerging Trends*, ed. R. S. Sugirtharajah (Maryknoll, N.Y.: Orbis Books, 1994), 80-89.

50. Gnanadason, "Women and Spirituality in Asia," 15-16.

51. Ibid., 17.

52. Dulcie Abraham, Sun Ai Lee Park, and Yvonne Dahlin, eds., *Faith Renewed: A Report on the First Asian Women's Consultation on Interfaith Dialogue* (Hong Kong: Asian Women's Resource Center for Culture and Theology, n.d.), 121.

53. Chung, *Struggle to Be the Sun Again*, 113.

6. Woman, Dogs, and Crumbs: Constructing a Postcolonial Discourse

1. See Ben Witherington III, *Women in the Ministry of Jesus: A Study of Jesus' Attitudes to Women and Their Roles as Reflected in His Earthly Life* (Cambridge: Cambridge University Press, 1987), 63.

2. Gayatri Chakravorty Spivak, *In Other Worlds: Essays in Cultural Politics* (New York: Methuen, 1987) and *The Post-Colonial Critic: Interviews, Strategies, Dialogues* (New York: Routledge, 1990).

3. Rudolf Bultmann classifies this story as one of the *apophthegms* and not a miracle story. See *The History of the Synoptic Traditions*, trans. John Marsh (Oxford: Basil Blackwell, 1963), 38, 63.

4. Mieke Bal, *Death and Dissymmetry: The Politics of Coherence in the Book of Judges* (Chicago: University of Chicago Press, 1988), 3. See also Elisabeth Schüssler Fiorenza, "Text and Reality—Reality as Text: The Problem of a Feminist Historical and Social Reconstruction Based on Texts," *Studia Theologica* 43 (1989): 19-34; Ched Myers, *Binding the Strong Man: A Political Reading of Mark's Story of Jesus* (Maryknoll, N.Y.: Orbis Books, 1988), 22-28.

5. Bal, *Death and Dissymmetry*, 248-49.

6. Bruce J. Malina and Richard L. Rohrbaugh, *Social-Science Commentary on the Synoptic Gospels* (Minneapolis: Fortress, 1992), 225.

7. Janice Capel Anderson, "Matthew: Gender and Reading," *Semeia* 28 (1983): 7-8.

8. David Rhoads, "Jesus and the Syrophoenician Woman in Mark: A Narrative-Critical Study," *Journal of the American Academy of Religion* 62 (1994): 358.

9. Deborah Tannen, *You Just Don't Understand: Women and Men in Conversation* (New York: William Morrow, 1990), 24-25. Tannen argues that women and men speak differently because of their unequal position in society. She does not subscribe to an essentialist view.

10. Ibid., 25.

11. Spivak, *The Post-Colonial Critic*, 73.

12. Elizabeth Struthers Malbon suggests that the foreignness of these cities is "more crucial in Mark's Gospel than their precise location or Jesus' exact itinerary in reaching them." See her *Narrative Space and Mythic Meaning in Mark* (San Francisco: Harper and Row, 1986), 41.

13. Elaine Mary Wainwright, *Towards a Feminist Critical Reading of the Gospel according to Matthew* (New York: Walter de Gruyter, 1991), 224-25.

14. Burton L. Mack, *A Myth of Innocence* (Philadelphia: Fortress, 1988), 214.

15. Vincent Taylor, *The Gospel According to St. Mark* (London: Macmillan, 1952), 350.

16. Francis Dufton, "The Syrophoenician Woman and Her Dogs," *Expository Times* 100 (November 1989): 417.

17. Witherington, *Women in the Ministry of Jesus*, 66; Antoinette Clark Wire, "Gender Roles in a Scribal Community," 104.

18. Mary Ann Tolbert, *Sowing the Gospel: Mark's World in Literary-Historical Perspective* (Minneapolis: Fortress, 1989), 185.

19. Anderson, "Matthew: Gender and Reading," 14.

20. T. A. Burkill, "The Historical Development of the Story of the Syrophoenician Woman (Mark 7: 24-31)," *Novem Testamentum* 9 (1967): 161-77.

21. Wainwright, *Towards a Feminist Critical Reading*, 240.

22. Gerd Theissen, *The Miracle Stories of the Early Christian Tradition*, trans. Francis McDonagh (Philadelphia: Fortress, 1983), 181-83. Theissen says the order is repeated four times in Matthew. Wainwright notes that the woman makes only three petitions and modifies his scheme. See *Towards a Feminist Critical Reading*, 219.

23. Antoinette Clark Wire, "The Structure of the Gospel Miracle Stories and Their Tellers," *Semeia* 11 (1978): 103.

24. See Schüssler Fiorenza, *But She Said*, 161.

25. The issue of displacement is discussed in Gayatri Chakravorty Spivak, "Can the Subaltern Speak?" in *Marxism and the Interpretation of Culture*, ed. Cary

Nelson and Lawrence Grossberg (Urbana: University of Illinois Press, 1988), 271-313.

26. Martin Luther, *Luther's Works* (hereafter refer to as *LW*) (St. Louis: Concordia Publishing House, 1970), 6:284-85.

27. *LW*, 6:262.

28. *LW*, 4:55.

29. *LW*, 17:400.

30. *LW*, 4:54.

31. *LW*, 41:51.

32. Nandy, *The Intimate Enemy*, 4.

33. See Charles Hartwell, *Zhengdao qimeng* (Enlightenment on truth) (Fuzhou: Taiping jie fuyin tang, 1871).

34. Mrs. Timothy Richard, "The Christian and the Chinese Idea of Womanhood and How Our Mission Schools May Help Them to Develop the Former Idea," *Chinese Recorder* 31 (1900): 11-12.

35. Kwok Pui-lan, "The Image of the 'White Lady': Gender and Race in Christian Mission," *Concilium*, 1991, no. 6:24.

36. Judith Plaskow, "Anti-Judaism in Feminist Christian Interpretation," in *A Feminist Introduction*, vol. 1 of *Searching the Scriptures*, 119.

37. Ibid., 123.

38. Renita J. Weems, "The Hebrew Women Are Not Like the Egyptian Women: The Ideology of Race, Gender and Sexual Reproduction in Exodus 1," *Semeia* 59 (1992): 32.

39. Hisako Kinukawa, *Women and Jesus in Mark: A Japanese Feminist Perspective* (Maryknoll, N.Y.: Orbis Books, 1994), 59.

40. Ibid., 61.

41. Sharon H. Ringe, "A Gentile Woman's Story," in *Feminist Interpretation of the Bible*, 70-72.

42. Rita Monteiro, Judith Sequeira, and Frances Yasas, "Waiting to Be Recognized," *In God's Image* (September 1988): 49.

43. Schüssler Fiorenza, *But She Said*, 97.

44. R. S. Sugirtharajah, "The Syrophoenician Woman," *Expository Times* 98 (October 1986): 14.

45. Ibid., 15.

46. Ringe, "A Gentile Woman's Story," 71, as quoted in Sugirtharajah, "Jesus and Mission: Some Redefinitions," in *The Scandal of the Cross: Evangelism and Mission Today*, ed. Wendy S. Robins and Gillian Hawney (London: The United Society for the Propagation of the Gospel, 1992), 3.

47. Sugirtharajah, "Jesus and Mission," 3.

48. Kwok Pui-lan, "Worshipping with Asian Women: A Homily on Jesus Healing the Daughter of a Canaanite Woman," in *Feminist Theology from the Third World*, ed. Ursula King (Maryknoll, N.Y.: Orbis Books, 1994), 239-40. This is from a sermon preached by Kesaya Noda, Kim Hee Sang, Paula K. R. Arai, and myself at Harvard Divinity School on February 19, 1986.

49. Gerd Theissen, *The Gospels in Context: Social and Political History in the Synoptic Tradition* (Minneapolis: Fortress, 1991), 68-75.

50. Kwok, "Worshipping with Asian Women," 237, 239.

7. Racism and Ethnocentrism in Feminist Biblical Interpretation

1. Teresa Okure, "Women in the Bible," in *With Passion and Compassion: Third World Women Doing Theology*, ed. Virginia Fabella and Mercy Amba Oduyoye (Maryknoll, N.Y.: Orbis Books, 1988), 56.

2. Elsa Tamez, "Women's Rereading of the Bible," in *With Passion and Compassion*, 176.

3. From Chapter 1, page 19, above.

4. Sheila Briggs, "Can an Enslaved God Liberate? Hermeneutical Reflections on Philippians 2:6-11," *Semeia* 47 (1989): 140.

5. See Sugirtharajah, *Voices from the Margin*, and Felder, *Stony the Road We Trod*. See also Wimbush, "Historical/Cultural Criticism as Liberation," 43-55; Schüssler Fiorenza, *Bread Not Stone*, 128-36.

6. Weems, "Reading *Her Way*," 66.

7. Ibid., 66; Ernesto Cardenal, *The Gospel in Solentiname*, 4 vols. (Maryknoll, N.Y.: Orbis Books, 1976-1982).

8. See Jacquelyn Grant, *White Women's Christ and Black Women's Jesus: Feminist Christology and Womanist Response* (Atlanta: Scholars Press, 1989), 211-12; and Weems, "Reading *Her Way*," 61-62.

9. Jarena Lee, "The Life and Religious Experience of Jarena Lee," in *Sisters of the Spirit: Three Black Women's Autobiographies of the Nineteenth Century*, ed. William L. Andrews (Bloomington: Indiana University Press, 1986), 36, quoted in Clarice J. Martin, "The *Haustafeln* (Household Code) in African American Biblical Interpretation: 'Free Slaves' and 'Subordinate Women,'" in *Stony the Road We Trod*, 222-23.

10. See "The History of Ms. Zhang Zhujun," in *Jindai Zhongguo nüquan yundong shiliao* (Historical materials on the modern Chinese feminist movement) (Taibei: Biographical Literature Publisher, 1975), 2:1380.

11. Elisabeth Schüssler Fiorenza, "The Politics of Otherness: Biblical Interpretation as a Critical Praxis for Liberation," in *The Future of Liberation Theology*, ed. Marc H. Ellis and Otto Maduro (Maryknoll, N.Y.: Orbis Books, 1989), 316.

12. Renita J. Weems, "Do You See What I See? Diversity in Interpretation," *Church and Society* 82:1 (September/October 1991): 40. See also her *Just a Sister Away: A Womanist Vision of Women's Relationships in the Bible* (San Diego: LuraMedia, 1988), 1-21.

13. Tamez, "The Woman Who Complicated the History of Salvation," 5-17.

14. Musimbi R. A. Kanyoro, "Interpreting Old Testament Polygamy through African Eyes," in *The Will to Arise: Women, Tradition, and the Church in Africa*, ed. Mercy Amba Oduyoye and Musimbi R. A. Kanyoro (Maryknoll, N.Y.: Orbis Books, 1992), 95.

15. Anne Nasimiyu-Wasike, "Polygamy: A Feminist Critique," in *The Will to Arise*, 110.

16. Philo, *De Abrahamo*, 251, as quoted in Gerd Theissen, *The Gospels in Context*, 69.

17. Briggs, "Can an Enslaved God Liberate?" 142. Her article has an excellent discussion on the use of analogy in historical reconstruction, see pages 139-42.

18. Judith Plaskow, "Anti-Judaism in Feminist Christian Interpretation," 117-29.

19. Plaskow, *Standing Again at Sinai*, 33.

20. Cain Hope Felder, "Race, Racism, and the Biblical Narratives," in *Stony the Road We Trod*, 137-38.

21. Katie Geneva Cannon, "Slave Ideology and Biblical Interpretation," *Semeia* 47 (1989): 11-13.

22. Clarice J. Martin, "A Chamberlain's Journey and the Challenge of Interpretation for Liberation," *Semeia* 47 (1989): 105-35.

23. Felder, "Race, Racism, and the Biblical Narratives," 136-37. See also Charles B. Copher, "The Black Presence in the Old Testament," in *Stony the Road We Trod*, 146-64.

24. Naim Stifan Ateek, "A Palestinian Perspective: The Bible and Liberation," in *Voices from the Margin*, 283.

25. Robert Allen Warrior, "A Native American Perspective: Canaanites, Cowboys, and Indians," in *Voices from the Margin*, 289.

26. Ibid., 293.

27. Sanneh, *Translating the Message*, 1.

28. Theissen, *The Gospels in Context*, 68-72.

29. Ibid., 79-80.

30. Rita Nakashima Brock, *Journeys by Heart: A Christology of Erotic Power* (New York: Crossroad, 1988), 84.

31. C. F. Andrew, ed., *Mahatma Gandhi: His Own Story* (London: George Allen and Unwin, 1930), 31, quoted by Sugirtharajah, "Inter-faith Hermeneutics," 352.

32. Kim Sung Hae, "The Righteous and the Sage: A Comparative Study of the Ideal Images of Man in Biblical Israel and Classical China" (Th.D. Diss., Harvard University, 1981).

33. Ishanand Vempeny, *Krsna and Christ: In the Light of Some of the Fundamental Themes and Concepts of the Bhagavad Gita and the New Testament* (Pune: Ishvani Kendra, 1988); John Eaton, *The Contemplative Face of the Old Testament in the Context of World Religions* (London: SCM, 1989).

34. Yagi, "'I' in the Words of Jesus," 117-34.

35. Weems, "Reading *Her Way*," 71.

36. See Rita Nakashima Brock, "Dusting the Bible on the Floor: A Hermeneutics of Wisdom," in *A Feminist Introduction*, vol. 1 of *Searching the Scriptures*, 69.

37. Martin, "The *Haustafeln*," 225.

38. Nasimiyu-Wasike, "Polygamy: A Feminist Critique," 114-15.

39. Weems, "Do You See What I See?" 28.

Epilogue

I would like to thank James and Louise Palm, former director and staff of the Stony Point Center, for their friendship and support.

1. Paul Monette, *Borrowed Time: An AIDS Memoir* (New York: Harcourt Brace Jovanovich, 1988).

2. Sugirtharajah, *Voices from the Margin*, 229-95.

3. Warrior, "A Native American Perspective," 289.

4. Ateek, "A Palestinian Perspective," 283.

5. Marc H. Ellis, *Toward a Jewish Theology of Liberation: The Uprising and the Future* (Maryknoll, N.Y.: Orbis Books, 1987).

6. Robert Jay Lifton, *The Future of Immortality and Other Essays for a Nuclear Age* (New York: Basic Books, 1987).

7. Ibid., 27.

SELECTED BIBLIOGRAPHY

Abraham, Dulcie, Sun Ai Lee Park, and Yvonne Dahlin, eds. *Faith Renewed: A Report on the First Asian Women's Consultation on Interfaith Dialogue*. Hong Kong: Asian Women's Resource Center for Culture and Theology, n.d.

Abraham, K. C., ed. *Third World Theologies: Commonalities and Divergences*. Maryknoll, N.Y.: Orbis Books, 1990.

Alcoff, Linda. "Cultural Feminism versus Post-Structuralism: The Identity Crisis in Feminist Theory." *Signs* 13 (1988): 405-36.

Amalorpavadass, D. S., ed. *Research Seminar on Non-Biblical Scriptures*. Bangalore: National Biblical, Catechetical, and Liturgical Center, 1974.

Anderson, Janice Capel. "Matthew: Gender and Reading." *Semeia* 28 (1983): 3-27.

Antone, Hope S., and Yong Tin Jin, eds. *Re-Living Our Faith Today: A Bible Study Resource Book*. Hong Kong: World Student Christian Federation, Asia-Pacific Region, 1992.

Ariarajah, Wesley. *The Bible and People of Other Faiths*. Maryknoll, N.Y.: Orbis Books, 1989.

Ashcroft, Bill, Gareth Griffiths, and Helen Tiffin. *The Empire Writes Back: Theory and Practice in Post-Colonial Literature*. London: Routledge, 1989.

Bach, Alice, ed. *The Pleasure of Her Text: Feminist Readings of Biblical and Historical Texts*. Philadelphia: Trinity Press International, 1990.

Bakhtin, M. M. *The Dialogic Imagination: Four Essays*. Edited by Michael Holquist. Austin: University of Texas Press, 1981.

_____ [V. N. Voloshinov, pseudo.]. *Marxism and the Philosophy of Language*. Translated by L. Matejka and I. R. Titunik. New York: Seminar Press, 1973.

Bal, Mieke. *Death and Dissymmetry: The Politics of Coherence in the Book of Judges*. Chicago: University of Chicago Press, 1988.

Barr, James. *Fundamentalism*. Philadelphia: Westminster, 1977.

_____ . "Story and History in Biblical Theology." *Journal of Religion* 56 (1976): 1-17.

Barrett, Michèle, and Anne Phillips, eds. *Destabilizing Theory: Contemporary Feminist Debates*. Stanford: Stanford University Press, 1992.

Briggs, Sheila. "Can an Enslaved God Liberate? Hermeneutical Reflections on Philippians 2:6-11." *Semeia* 47 (1989): 137-53.

_____ . "The Deceit of the Sublime: An Investigation into the Origins of Ideological Criticism of the Bible in Early Nineteenth-Century German Biblical Studies." *Semeia* 59 (1992): 1-23.

_____ . "The Politics of Identity and the Politics of Interpretation." *Union Seminary Quarterly Review* 43 (1989): 163-80.

Brock, Rita Nakashima. *Journeys by Heart: A Christology of Erotic Power*. New York: Crossroad, 1988.

Bultmann, Rudolf. *The History of the Synoptic Traditions*. Translated by John Marsh. Oxford: Basil Blackwell, 1963.

Burkill, T. A. "The Historical Development of the Story of the Syrophoenician Woman (Mark 7:24-31)." *Novum Testamentum* 9 (1967): 161-77.

Cannon, Katie Geneva. *Black Womanist Ethics*. Atlanta: Scholars Press, 1988.

———. "Slave Ideology and Biblical Interpretation." *Semeia* 47 (1989): 9-23.

Cardenal, Ernesto. *The Gospel in Solentiname*. 4 vols. Maryknoll, N.Y.: Orbis Books, 1976-1982.

Carroll, David. "The Alterity of Discourse: Form, History, and the Question of the Political in M. M. Bakhtin." *Diacritics* 13:2 (Summer 1993): 65-83.

Chang, Tung-sun. "A Chinese Philosopher's Theory of Knowledge." *Yenching Journal of Social Studies* 1:2 (1939): 155-91.

Chao, T. C. "The Articulate Word and the Problem of Communication." *International Review of Mission* 36 (1947): 482-89.

———. "Revelation." In *The Authority of the Faith*. New York: International Missionary Council, 1939.

Chao, Yen Ren. *Aspects of Chinese Sociolinguistics*. Stanford: Stanford University Press, 1976.

Chen, Chi-yun. "Chinese Language and Truth—A Critique of Chad Hansen's Analysis." *Chinese Culture Quarterly* 31:2 (1990): 53-80.

Chen, Ellen M. *The Tao Te Ching: A New Translation with Commentary*. New York: Paragon House, 1989.

Choi, Man Ja. "Feminine Images of God in Korean Traditional Religion." In *Frontiers in Asian Christian Theology: Emerging Trends*, edited by R. S. Sugirtharajah. Maryknoll, N.Y.: Orbis Books, 1994.

Chopp, Rebecca S. *The Power to Speak: Feminism, Language, God*. New York: Crossroad, 1989.

Christ, Carol P. *Laughter of Aphrodite: Reflection on a Journey to the Goddess*. San Francisco: Harper and Row, 1987.

———, and Judith Plaskow, eds. *Womanspirit Rising: A Feminist Reader in Religion*. San Francisco: Harper and Row, 1979.

Christensen, Torben, and William R. Hutchison, eds. *Missionary Ideologies in the Imperialist Era: 1880-1920*. Arthus, Denmark: Aros, 1982.

Christian, Barbara. *Black Feminist Criticism: Perspectives on Black Women Writers*. New York: Pergamon, 1985.

Chung, Hyun Kyung. "Come, Holy Spirit—Renew the Whole Creation." In *Signs of the Spirit: Official Report, Seventh Assembly*, edited by Michael Kinnamon. Geneva: World Council of Churches, 1991.

———. *Struggle to Be the Sun Again: Introducing Asian Women's Theology*. Maryknoll, N.Y.: Orbis Books, 1990.

Cohen, Paul A. *Discovering History in China: American Historical Writings on the Recent Chinese Past*. New York: Columbia University Press, 1984.

Collins, Adela Yarbro, ed. *Feminist Perspectives on Biblical Scholarship*. Atlanta: Scholars Press, 1985.

Collins, Patricia Hill. *Black Feminist Thought: Knowledge, Consciousness, and the Politics of Empowerment.* London: HarperCollins Academic, 1990.

Cone, James H. *A Black Theology of Liberation.* 2d ed. Maryknoll, N.Y.: Orbis Books, 1990.

Coward, Harold. *Sacred Word and Sacred Text: Scripture in World Religions.* Maryknoll, N.Y.: Orbis Books, 1988.

Culler, Jonathan. *On Deconstruction: Theory and Criticism after Structuralism.* Ithaca, N.Y.: Cornell University Press, 1982.

Deleuze, Gilles, and Félix Guattari. "What Is a Minor Literature?" *Mississippi Review* 22:3 (1983): 13-33.

Denny, Frederick M., and Rodney L. Taylor, eds. *The Holy Book in Comparative Perspective.* Columbia, S.C.: University of South Carolina Press, 1985.

Derrida, Jacques. *Of Grammatology.* Translated by Gayatri Chakravorty Spivak. Baltimore: Johns Hopkins University Press, 1974.

Detweiler, Robert. "What Is a Sacred Text?" *Semeia* 31 (1985): 213-30.

Dewey, Joanna. "Feminist Readings, Gospel Narrative and Critical Theory." *Biblical Theology Bulletin* 22:4 (1992): 167-73.

_____. "From Storytelling to the Written Text: The Loss of Early Christian Women's Voices." Unpublished paper.

_____. "Mark as Interwoven Tapestry: Forecasts and Echoes for a Listening Audience." *Catholic Biblical Quarterly* 53 (1991): 221-36.

_____. "Oral Methods of Structuring Narrative in Mark." *Interpretation* 43 (1989): 32-44.

Drego, Pearl. "Annunciation." *In God's Image* (December 1989): 11-14.

Dufton, Francis. "The Syrophoenician Woman and Her Dogs." *Expository Times* 100 (November 1989): 417.

Duraisingh, Christopher. "Reflection on Theological Hermeneutics in the Indian Context." *Indian Journal of Theology* 31:3-4 (1982): 259-78.

Eaton, John. *The Contemplative Face of the Old Testament in the Context of World Religions.* London: SCM, 1989.

EATWOT Women in the Philippines and Asia. *Toward an Asian Principle of Interpretation: A Filipino Women's Experience.* Manila: Ecumenical Association of Third World Theologians, 1991.

Ellis, Marc H. *Toward a Jewish Theology of Liberation: The Uprising and the Future.* Maryknoll, N.Y.: Orbis Books, 1987.

Ellsberg, Robert, ed. *Gandhi on Christianity.* Maryknoll, N.Y.: Orbis Books, 1991.

Elwood, Douglas J., ed. *Asian Christian Theology: Emerging Themes.* Philadelphia: Westminster, 1980.

England, John C., and Archie C. C. Lee, eds. *Doing Theology with Asian Resources: Ten Years in the Formation of Living Theology in Asia.* Hong Kong: Program for Theology and Cultures in Asia, 1993.

Fabella, Virginia. *Beyond Bonding: A Third World Women's Theological Journey.* Manila: Ecumenical Association of Third World Theologians, 1993.

_____, and Mercy Amba Oduyoye, eds. *With Passion and Compassion: Third World Women Doing Theology.* Maryknoll, N.Y.: Orbis Books, 1988.

_____, and Sun Ai Lee Park, eds. *We Dare to Dream: Doing Theology as Asian Women.* Maryknoll, N.Y.: Orbis Books, 1989.

_____ , Peter K. H. Lee, and David Kwang-sun Suh, eds. *Asian Christian Spirituality: Reclaiming Traditions.* Maryknoll, N.Y.: Orbis Books, 1992.

Felder, Cain Hope. "Afrocentrism and Biblical Authority." *Theology Today* 49 (1992): 357-66.

_____ , ed. *Stony the Road We Trod: African American Biblical Interpretation.* Minneapolis: Fortress, 1991.

Foucault, Michel. *Power/Knowledge: Selected Interviews and Other Writings, 1972-1977.* Edited by Colin Gordon. New York: Pantheon Books, 1980.

Frei, Hans W. *The Eclipse of Biblical Narrative: A Study of Eighteenth and Nineteenth Century Hermeneutics.* New Haven: Yale University Press, 1974.

Fulkerson, Mary McClintock. *Changing the Subject: Women's Discourses and Feminist Theology.* Minneapolis: Fortress, 1994.

Gallup, Padma. "Doing Theology—An Asian Feminist Perspective." *Commission on Theological Concerns Bulletin, Christian Conference of Asia* 4 (1983): 21-27.

Gates, Henry Louis, Jr. *The Signifying Monkey: A Theory of African-American Literary Criticism.* New York: Oxford University Press, 1988.

_____ , ed. *"Race," Writing, and Difference.* Chicago: University of Chicago Press, 1985.

Gilkes, Cheryl Townsend. "'Mother to the Motherless, Father to the Fatherless': Power, Gender, and Community in an Afrocentric Biblical Tradition." *Semeia* 47 (1989): 57-85.

Gilmartin, Christina K., Gail Hershatter, Lisa Rofel, and Tyrene White, eds. *Engendering China: Women, Culture, and the State.* Cambridge, Mass.: Harvard University Press, 1994.

Gnanadason, Aruna. "Feminist Theology: An Indian Perspective." *In God's Image* (December 1988): 44-51.

_____ . "A Spirituality that Sustains Us in Our Struggles." *International Review of Mission* 80 (1991): 29-41.

_____ . "Women and Spirituality in Asia." *In God's Image* (December 1989): 15-18.

Goody, Jack. *The Interface between the Written and the Oral.* Cambridge: Cambridge University Press, 1987.

Gottwald, Norman K., and Richard A. Horsley, eds. *The Bible and Liberation: Political and Social Hermeneutics.* rev. ed. Maryknoll, N.Y.: Orbis Books, 1993.

Graham, Susan Lochrie. "Silent Voices: Women in the Gospel of Mark." *Semeia* 54 (1991): 145-58.

Graham, William A. *Beyond the Written Word: Oral Aspects of Scripture in the History of Religion.* Cambridge: Cambridge University Press, 1987.

Grant, Jacquelyn. *White Women's Christ and Black Women's Jesus: Feminist Christology and Womanist Response.* Atlanta: Scholars Press, 1989.

Gregorios, Paulos. "The Hermeneutical Discussion in India Today." *Indian Journal of Theology* 31:3-4 (1982): 153-55.

Gross, Rita M. *Buddhism after Patriarchy: A Feminist History, Analysis, and Reconstruction of Buddhism.* Albany, N.Y.: State University of New York Press, 1993.

Hansen, Chad. "Chinese Ideographs and Western Ideas." *Journal of Asian Studies* 52 (1993): 373-99.

_____. "Chinese Language, Chinese Philosophy, and 'Truth.'" *Journal of Asian Studies* 44 (1985): 491-519.

Harper, Philip Brian. *Framing the Margins: The Social Logic of Postmodern Culture*. New York: Oxford University Press, 1994.

Henderson, John B. *Scripture, Canon, and Commentary: A Comparison of Confucian and Western Exegesis*. Princeton: Princeton University Press, 1991.

Henderson, Mae Gwendolyn. "Speaking in Tongues: Dialogics, Dialectics, and the Black Woman Writer's Literary Tradition." In *Reading Black, Reading Feminist: A Critical Anthology*, edited by Henry Louis Gates, Jr. New York: Meridian Books, 1990.

Higginbotham, Evelyn Brooks. "African-American Women's History and the Metalanguage of Race." *Signs* 17 (1992): 251-74.

_____. *Righteous Discontent: The Women's Movement in the Black Baptist Church, 1880-1920*. Cambridge, Mass.: Harvard University Press, 1993.

Hirsch, Marianne, and Evelyn Fox Keller, eds. *Conflicts in Feminism*. New York: Routledge, 1990.

Hirschkop, Ken, and David Shepherd, eds. *Bakhtin and Cultural Theory*. Manchester: Manchester University Press, 1989.

Ho, Winnie, ed. *Towards a Chinese Feminist Theology*. Hong Kong: Lutheran Theological Seminary, 1988.

hooks, bell. *Feminist Theory: From Margin to Center*. Boston: South End Press, 1984.

_____. *Yearning: Race, Gender, and Cultural Politics*. Boston: South End Press, 1990.

Isasi-Díaz, Ada María. *En la Lucha/In the Struggle: An Hispanic Women's Theology*. Minneapolis: Fortress, 1993.

James, Stanlie M., and Abena P. A. Busia, eds. *Theorizing Black Feminisms: The Visionary Pragmatism of Black Women*. New York: Routledge, 1993.

Jameson, Fredric. *The Political Unconscious: Narrative as a Socially Symbolic Art*. Ithaca, N.Y.: Cornell University Press, 1981.

JanMohamed, Abdul R., and David Lloyd, eds. *The Nature and Context of Minority Discourse*. New York: Oxford University Press, 1990.

Jobling, David. "Writing the Wrongs of the World: The Deconstruction of the Biblical Text in the Context of Liberation Theologies." *Semeia* 51 (1990): 81-118.

John, Crescy, Susan, Sun Ai Lee Park, Pearl Drego, Pauline, Mary Lobo, and Margaret Shanti. "The Exodus Story." *In God's Image* (September 1988): 43-48.

John, E. C. "Israel and Inculturation: An Appraisal." *Jeevadhara* 14 (1984): 87-94.

Katoppo, Marianne. *Compassionate and Free: An Asian Woman's Theology*. Geneva: World Council of Churches, 1979.

Kelber, Werner H. *The Oral and the Written Gospel: The Hermeneutics of Speaking and Writing in the Synoptic Tradition, Mark, Paul, and Q*. Philadelphia: Fortress, 1983.

Kim, C. W. Maggie, Susan M. St. Ville, and Susan M. Simonaitis, eds. *Transfigurations: Theology and the French Feminists*. Minneapolis: Fortress, 1993.

Kim, Sung Hae. "The Righteous and the Sage: A Comparative Study of the Ideal Images of Man in Biblical Israel and Classical China." Th.D. diss., Harvard University, 1981.

Kim, Yong Bock. "Minjung Social Biography and Theology." *Ching Feng* 28:4 (1985): 221-31.

―――, ed. *Minjung Theology: People as the Subjects of History*. Singapore: Commission on Theological Concerns, Christian Conference of Asia, 1981.

King, Deborah K. "Multiple Jeopardy, Multiple Consciousness: The Context of a Black Feminist Ideology." *Signs* 14 (1988): 42-72.

King, Ursula, ed. *Feminist Theology from the Third World*. Maryknoll, N.Y.: Orbis Books, 1994.

Kinukawa, Hisako. *Women and Jesus in Mark: A Japanese Feminist Perspective*. Maryknoll, N.Y.: Orbis Books, 1994.

Koonthanam, George. "The Prophets and the Nations." *Jeevadhara* 14 (1984): 123-35.

Koyama, Kosuke. *Mount Fuji and Mount Sinai: A Critique of Idols*. Maryknoll, N.Y.: Orbis Books, 1984.

―――. *No Handle on the Cross*. Maryknoll, N.Y.: Orbis Books, 1977.

―――. *Three Mile an Hour God*. Maryknoll, N.Y.: Orbis Books, 1980.

Kraemer, Hendrik. *The Christian Message in a Non-Christian World*. 3d ed. Grand Rapids, Mich.: Kregel, 1956.

Krieger, Murray, ed. *The Aims of Representation: Subject/Text/History*. Stanford: Stanford University Press, 1993.

Kristeva, Julia. *Language: The Unknown, an Initiation into Linguistics*. Translated by Anne M. Menke. New York: Columbia University Press, 1989.

Kwok, Pui-lan, "A Chinese Perspective." In *Theology by the People: Reflections on Doing Theology in Community*, edited by Samuel Amirtham and John S. Pobee. Geneva: World Council of Churches, 1986.

―――. *Chinese Women and Christianity, 1860-1927*. Atlanta: Scholars Press, 1992.

―――. "Discovering the Bible in the Non-Biblical World." *Semeia* 47 (1989): 25-42.

―――. "The Feminist Hermeneutics of Elisabeth Schüssler Fiorenza: An Asian Feminist Response." *East Asia Journal of Theology* 3:2 (1985): 147-53.

―――. "God Weeps with Our Pain." *East Asia Journal of Theology* 2:2 (1984): 228-32.

―――. "The Image of the 'White Lady': Gender and Race in Christian Mission." *Concilium*, 1991, no. 6:19-27.

―――. "Worshipping with Asian Women: A Homily on Jesus Healing the Daughter of a Canaanite Woman." In *Feminist Theology from the Third World*, edited by Ursula King. Maryknoll, N.Y.: Orbis, 1994.

Lam, Wing-hung, ed. *Jindai huaren shenxue wenxian* (A source book of modern Chinese theology). Hong Kong: China Graduate School of Theology, 1986.

Lau, D. C. *Lao Tzu: Tao Te Ching*. New York: Penguin Books, 1963.

Lee, Archie C. C. "Biblical Interpretation in Asian Perspectives." *Asia Journal of Theology* 7:1 (1993): 35-39.

―――. "The Chinese Creation Myth of Nu Kua and the Biblical Narrative in Genesis 1-11." *Biblical Interpretation* 2:3 (1994): 312-24.

Lee, Oo Chung et al., eds. *Women of Courage: Asian Women Reading the Bible*. Seoul: Asian Women's Resource Center for Culture and Theology, 1992.

Lee, Sung-hee. "Women's Liberation Theology as the Foundation for Asian Theology." *East Asia Journal of Theology* 4:2 (1986): 2-13.

Levering, Miriam, ed. *Rethinking Scripture: Essays from a Comparative Perspective.* Albany, N.Y.: State University of New York Press, 1989.

Lewis, Nantawan Boonprasat. "Asian Women's Theology: A Historical and Theological Analysis." *East Asia Journal of Theology* 4:2 (1986): 18-22.

_____ , ed. *An Ocean with Many Shores: Asian Women Making Connections in Theology and Ministry.* New York: Asian Women Theologians, Northeast U. S. Group, 1987.

Lohr, Charles H. "Oral Techniques in the Gospel of Matthew." *Catholic Biblical Quarterly* 23 (1961): 403-35.

Lorde, Audre. *Sister Outsider.* Trumansburg, N.Y.: Crossing Press, 1984.

Lu, Tonglin, ed. *Gender and Sexuality in Twentieth-Century Chinese Literature and Society.* Albany, N.Y.: State University of New York Press, 1993.

Mack, Burton L. *A Myth of Innocence.* Philadelphia: Fortress, 1988.

Malbon, Elizabeth Struthers. *Narrative Space and Mythic Meaning in Mark.* San Francisco: Harper and Row, 1986.

Malina, Bruce J., and Richard L. Rohrbaugh. *Social-Science Commentary on the Synoptic Gospels.* Minneapolis: Fortress, 1992.

Martin, Clarice J. "A Chamberlain's Journey and the Challenge of Interpretation for Liberation." *Semeia* 47 (1989): 105-35.

McConnell, Frank, ed. *The Bible and the Narrative Tradition.* New York: Oxford University Press, 1986.

McFague, Sallie. *Metaphorical Theology: Models of God in Religious Language.* Philadelphia: Fortress, 1982.

Monteiro, Rita, Judith Sequeira, and Frances Yasas. "Waiting to Be Recognized." *In God's Image* (September 1988): 49-50.

Moon, Cyris H. S. *A Korean Minjung Theology: An Old Testament Perspective.* Maryknoll, N.Y.: Orbis Books, 1985.

Moore, Stephen D. "The 'Post-'Age Stamp: Does it Stick? Biblical Studies and the Postmodernism Debate." *Journal of the American Academy of Religion* 57 (1989): 543-59.

Mosala, Itumeleng J. *Biblical Hermeneutics and Black Theology in South Africa.* Grand Rapids, Mich.: William B. Eerdmans, 1989.

_____ . "The Implications of the Text of Esther for African Women's Struggle for Liberation in South Africa." *Semeia* 59 (1992): 129-37.

Mott, John R. *The Evangelization of the World in This Generation.* 1900. Reprint. New York: Arno Books, 1972.

Muslim-Christian Research Group. *The Challenge of the Scriptures: The Bible and the Qur'an.* Maryknoll, N.Y.: Orbis Books, 1989.

Myers, Ched. *Binding the Strong Man: A Political Reading of Mark's Story of Jesus.* Maryknoll, N.Y.: Orbis Books, 1988.

Nandy, Ashis. *The Intimate Enemy: Loss and Recovery of Self under Colonialism.* Delhi: Oxford University Press, 1983.

Ng, Lee-ming, "The Promise and Limitations of Chinese Protestant Theologians, 1920-1950." *Ching Feng* 21:4-22:1 (1978-1979): 175-82.

Niles, D. Preman. "Examples of Contextualization in the Old Testament." *South East Asia Journal of Theology* 21:2-22:1 (1980-1981): 19-33.

————. "Story and Theology—A Proposal." *East Asia Journal of Theology* 3:1 (1985): 112-26.

————. "The Word of God and the People of Asia." In *Understanding the Word: Essays in Honor of Bernhard W. Anderson*, edited by James T. Butler, Edgar W. Conrad, and Ben C. Ollenburger. Sheffield: Journal for the Study of the Old Testament, 1985.

O'Flaherty, Wendy Doniger. "The Uses and Misuses of Other Peoples' Myths." *Journal of the American Academy of Religion* 54 (1986): 219-39.

Oduyoye, Mercy Amba, and Musimbi R. A. Kanyoro, eds. *The Will to Arise: Women, Tradition, and the Church in Africa*. Maryknoll, N.Y.: Orbis Books, 1992.

Olson, David R. "From Utterance to Text: The Bias of Language in Speech and Writing." *Harvard Educational Review* 47:3 (1977): 257-81.

————, and Nancy Torrance, eds. *Literacy and Orality*. Cambridge: Cambridge University Press, 1991.

Ong, Walter J. *The Presence of the Word: Some Prolegomena for Cultural and Religious History*. New Haven: Yale University Press, 1967.

————. "Text as Interpretation: Mark and After." *Semeia* 39 (1987): 7-26.

Oracion, Levi V. "Theological Reflections on Indarapatra and S. Sulayman." *East Asia Journal of Theology* 3:2 (1985): 213-21.

Park, Sun Ai Lee. "Understanding the Bible from Women's Perspective." *Voices from the Third World* 10:2 (1987): 66-75.

Petersen, Norman R. *Literary Criticism for New Testament Critics*. Philadelphia: Fortress, 1978.

Pieris, Aloysius. *An Asian Theology of Liberation*. Maryknoll, N.Y.: Orbis Books, 1988.

Plaskow, Judith. *Standing Again at Sinai: Judaism from a Feminist Perspective*. San Francisco: Harper and Row, 1990.

Pobee, John S., and Bärbel von Wartenberg-Potter, eds. *New Eyes for Reading: Biblical and Theological Reflections by Women from the Third World*. Oak Parks, Ill.: Meyer Stone Books, 1987.

Poland, Lynn M. *Literary Criticism and Biblical Hermeneutics: A Critique of Formalist Approaches*. Chico, Calif.: Scholars Press, 1985.

Pongudom, Maen. "Creation of Man: Theological Reflections Based on Northern Thai Folktales." *East Asia Journal of Theology* 3:2 (1985): 222-27.

Ramanujan, A. K. "Tell It to the Walls: On Folktales in Indian Culture." In *India Briefing, 1992*, edited by L. A. Gordon and P. Oldenburg. Boulder: Westview, 1992.

Ramsey, S. Robert. *The Languages of China*. Princeton: Princeton University Press, 1987.

Rhoads, David. "Jesus and the Syrophoenician Woman in Mark: A Narrative-Critical Study." *Journal of the American Academy of Religion* 62 (1994): 343-75.

Ringe, Sharon H. "The Word of God May Be Hazardous to Your Health." *Theology Today* 49 (1992): 367-75.

Ruether, Rosemary Radford. *Womanguides: Reading Toward a Feminist Theology.* Boston: Beacon, 1985.

Russell, Letty, ed. *Feminist Interpretation of the Bible.* Philadelphia: Westminster, 1985.

Said, Edward W. *Orientalism.* New York: Pantheon Books, 1978.

_____. *The World, the Text, and the Critic.* Cambridge, Mass.: Harvard University Press, 1983.

Sakenfeld, Katherine Doob. "Feminist Perspectives on Bible and Theology: An Introduction to Selected Issues and Literature." *Interpretation* 42 (1988): 5-18.

Samartha, Stanley J. *Courage for Dialogue: Ecumenical Issues in Inter-Religious Relationships.* Geneva: World Council of Churches, 1981.

_____. "The Cross and the Rainbow: Christ in a Multireligious Culture." In *The Myth of Christian Uniqueness: Toward a Pluralistic Theology of Religions,* edited by John Hick and Paul F. Knitter. Maryknoll, N.Y.: Orbis Books, 1987.

_____. *One Christ—Many Religions: Toward a Revised Christology.* Maryknoll, N.Y.: Orbis Books, 1991.

_____. "Religion, Language and Reality: Towards a Relational Hermeneutics." *Biblical Interpretation* 2:3 (1994): 340-62.

_____. *The Search for New Hermeneutics in Asian Christian Theology.* Madras: Christian Literature Society, 1987.

Sanneh, Lamin. *Encountering the West: Christianity and the Global Cultural Process.* Maryknoll, N.Y.: Orbis Books, 1993.

_____. *Translating the Message: The Missionary Impact on Culture.* Maryknoll, N.Y.: Orbis Books, 1990.

Schneiders, Sandra M. *The Revelatory Text: Interpreting the New Testament as Sacred Literature.* San Francisco: Harper SanFrancisco, 1991.

Schüssler Fiorenza, Elisabeth. *Bread Not Stone: The Challenge of Feminist Biblical Interpretation.* Boston: Beacon, 1984.

_____. *But She Said: Feminist Practices of Biblical Interpretation.* Boston: Beacon, 1992.

_____. "The Ethics of Interpretation: De-Centering Biblical Scholarship." *Journal of Biblical Literature* 107 (1988): 3-17.

_____. *In Memory of Her: A Feminist Theological Reconstruction of Christian Origins.* New York: Crossroad, 1983.

_____. "The Politics of Otherness: Biblical Interpretation as a Critical Praxis for Liberation." In *The Future of Liberation Theology,* edited by Marc H. Ellis and Otto Maduro. Maryknoll, N.Y.: Orbis Books, 1989.

_____. "Text and Reality—Reality as Text: The Problem of a Feminist Historical and Social Reconstruction Based on Texts." *Studia Theologica* 43 (1989): 19-34.

_____, ed. *Searching the Scriptures.* Vol. 1, *A Feminist Introduction.* New York: Crossroad, 1993.

Schüssler Fiorenza, Francis. "The Crisis of Scriptural Authority: Interpretation and Reception." *Interpretation* 44 (1990): 353-68.

Schwartz, Benjamin I. *The World of Thought in Ancient China.* Cambridge, Mass.: Belknap Press, 1985.

Showalter, Elaine, ed. *Feminist Criticism: Essays on Women, Literature, Theory.* New York: Pantheon Books, 1985.

Smith, Wilfred Cantwell. *What Is Scripture? A Comparative Approach.* Minneapolis: Fortress, 1993.

Soares-Prabhu, George M. "From Alienation to Inculturation: Some Reflections on Doing Theology in India Today." In *Bread and Breath: Essays in Honor of Samuel Ryan, S.J.*, edited by T. K. John. Anand, Gujarat: Gujarat Sahitya Prakash, 1991.

_____ . "The Historical Critical Method: Reflections on Its Relevance for the Study of the Gospels in India Today." In *Theologizing in India*, edited by M. Amaladoss, T. K. John, and G. Gispert-Sauch. Bangalore: Theological Publications in India, 1981.

_____ . "Two Mission Commands: An Interpretation of Matthew 28:16-20 in the Light of a Buddhist Text." *Biblical Interpretation* 2:3 (1994): 264-82.

Song, C. S. "From Israel to Asia: A Theological Leap." *Ecumenical Review* 28 (1976): 252-65.

_____ . *Jesus and the Reign of God.* Minneapolis: Fortress, 1993.

_____ . *Jesus, the Crucified People.* New York: Crossroad, 1990.

_____ . *The Tears of Lady Meng.* Geneva: World Council of Churches, 1981.

_____ . *Tell Us Our Names: Story Theology from an Asian Perspective.* Maryknoll, N.Y.: Orbis Books, 1984.

_____ . *Theology from the Womb of Asia.* Maryknoll, N.Y.: Orbis Books, 1986.

Spelman, Elizabeth V. *Inessential Women: Problems of Exclusion in Feminist Thought.* Boston: Beacon, 1988.

Spivak, Gayatri Chakravorty. "Can the Subaltern Speak?" In *Marxism and the Interpretation of Culture*, edited by Cary Nelson and Lawrence Grossberg. Urbana: University of Illinois Press, 1988.

_____ . *In Other Worlds: Essays in Cultural Politics.* New York: Methuen, 1987.

_____ . *Outside in the Teaching Machine.* New York: Routledge, 1993.

_____ . *The Post-Colonial Critic: Interviews, Strategies, Dialogues.* New York: Routledge, 1990.

Stendahl, Krister. "The Bible as a Classic and the Bible as Holy Scripture." *Journal of Biblical Literature* 103 (1984): 3-10.

Sugirtharajah, R. S. "The Bible and Its Asian Readers." *Biblical Interpretation* 1:1 (1993): 54-66.

_____ . "Jesus and Mission: Some Redefinitions." In *The Scandal of the Cross: Evangelism and Mission Today*, edited by Wendy S. Robins and Gillian Hawney. London: The United Society for the Propagation of the Gospel, 1992.

_____ . "The Syrophoenician Woman." *Expository Times* 98 (October 1986): 13-15.

_____ . "'What Do Men Say Remains of Me?': Current Jesus Research and Third World Christologies." *Asia Journal of Theology* 5:2 (1991): 331-37.

_____ , ed. *Voices from the Margin: Interpreting the Bible in the Third World.* Maryknoll, N.Y.: Orbis Books, 1991.

Suh, Nam Dong. "Cultural Theology, Political Theology and Minjung Theology." *Commission on Theological Concerns Bulletin, Christian Conference of Asia* 5:3-6:1 (1984-1985): 12-15.

Tannen, Deborah. *You Just Don't Understand: Women and Men in Conversation.* New York: William Morrow, 1990.

———, ed. *Spoken and Written Language: Exploring Orality and Literacy.* Norwood, N.J.: Ablex, 1982.

Taylor, Vincent. *The Gospel According to St. Mark.* London: Macmillan, 1952.

Theissen, Gerd. *The Gospels in Context: Social and Political History in the Synoptic Tradition.* Translated by Linda M. Maloney. Minneapolis: Fortress, 1991.

———. *The Miracle Stories of the Early Christian Tradition.* Translated by Francis McDonagh. Philadelphia: Fortress, 1983.

Thistlethwaite, Susan Brooks, and Mary Porter Engel, eds. *Lift Every Voice: Constructing Christian Theologies from the Underside.* San Francisco: Harper and Row, 1990.

Thomas, M. M. *The Acknowledged Christ of the Indian Renaissance.* London: SCM, 1969.

Tolbert, Mary Ann. *Sowing the Gospel: Mark's World in Literary-Historical Perspective.* Minneapolis: Fortress, 1989.

———, ed. "The Bible and Feminist Hermeneutics." *Semeia* 28 (1983).

Torres, Sergio, and John Eagleson, eds. *The Challenge of Basic Christian Communities.* Maryknoll, N.Y.: Orbis Books, 1981.

Tracy, David. *The Analogical Imagination: Christian Theology and the Culture of Pluralism.* New York: Crossroad, 1981.

Trible, Phyllis. *Texts of Terror: Literary-Feminist Readings of Biblical Narratives.* Philadelphia: Fortress, 1984.

Tu, Wei-ming. *Confucian Thought: Selfhood as Creative Transformation.* Albany, N.Y.: State University of New York Press, 1985.

Vempeny, Ishanand. *Krsna and Christ: In the Light of Some of the Fundamental Themes and Concepts of the Bhagavad Gita and the New Testament.* Pune: Ishvani Kendra, 1988.

Wainwright, Elaine Mary. *Towards a Feminist Critical Reading of the Gospel According to Matthew.* New York: Walter de Gruyter, 1991.

Waley, Arthur. *The Analects of Confucius.* London: George Allen and Unwin, 1938.

Wang, Weifan. "The Bible in Chinese." *China Theological Review* 8 (1993): 100-23.

Weems, Renita J. "Do You See What I See? Diversity in Interpretation." *Church and Society* 82:1 (September/October 1991): 28-43.

———. "The Hebrew Women Are Not Like the Egyptian Women: The Ideology of Race, Gender and Sexual Reproduction in Exodus 1." *Semeia* 59 (1992): 25-34.

———. *Just a Sister Away: A Womanist Vision of Women's Relationships in the Bible.* San Diego, Calif.: LuraMedia, 1988.

West, Cornel. *Beyond Eurocentrism and Multiculturalism.* Vol. 1, *Prophetic Thought in Postmodern Times.* Monroe, Maine: Common Courage Press, 1993.

———. *Keeping Faith: Philosophy and Race in America.* New York: Routledge, 1993.

Williams, Delores S. *Sisters in the Wilderness: The Challenge of Womanist Theology.* Maryknoll, N.Y.: Orbis Books, 1993.

Wimbush, Vincent L. "Historical/Cultural Criticism as Liberation: A Proposal for an African American Biblical Hermeneutic." *Semeia* 47 (1989): 43-55.

Wire, Antoinette Clark. "Gender Roles in a Scribal Community." In *Social History of the Matthean Community*, edited by David L. Balch. Minneapolis: Fortress, 1991.

————. "The Structure of the Gospel Miracle Stories and Their Tellers." *Semeia* 11 (1978): 83-113.

Witherington, Ben, III. *Women in the Ministry of Jesus: A Study of Jesus' Attitudes to Women and Their Roles as Reflected in His Earthly Life*. Cambridge: Cambridge University Press, 1987.

Women's Concerns Unit, Christian Conference of Asia, ed. *Reading the Bible as Asian Women*. Singapore: Christian Conference of Asia, 1986.

Wu, Y. T. "The Orient Reconsiders Christianity." *Christian Century* 54 (1937): 835-38.

Yagi, Seiichi. "'I' in the Words of Jesus." In *The Myth of Christian Uniqueness*, edited by John Hick and Paul F. Knitter. Maryknoll, N.Y.: Orbis Books, 1987.

Yeo, Khiok-khng. "The Rhetorical Hermeneutic of 1 Corinthians 8 and Chinese Ancestor Worship." *Biblical Interpretation* 2:3 (1994): 294-311.

Yeow, Choo Lak, ed. *Doing Theology with Cultures of Asia*. Singapore: Association for Theological Education in South East Asia, 1988.

Yuasa, Yuko. "The Spirit Moves through the Spirits in Noh Drama: A Study of the Man-Woman Relationship." In *Doing Theology with the Spirit's Movement in Asia*, edited by John C. England and Alan J. Torrance. Singapore: Association for Theological Education in South East Asia, 1991.

Yü, Ying-shih. *Lishi yu sixiang* (History and thought). Taibei: Linjing Publisher, 1976.

INDEX

136   INDEX

tion, 60; liberation and, 14; *min-jung*, 15-16, 170; multiple sources for, 17-18, 28-30; use of Bible in, 28-31

Thought, language and, 34-36

Tiananmen, ix-xvi, 55, 96, 97

Tradition: Asian hermeneutical, 27-28; Neo-Confucian, 11-12

Traditions: Asian, 14; faith, 92-93

Trible, Phyllis, 53

Truth: concept of, 35; hermeneutics and, 68; power and, 9-12

Vedas, 45-46

Wainwright, Elaine Mary, 74-75

War, Gulf, 96, 97

Warrior, Robert Allen, 91, 98

Weems, Renita J., 43, 44, 79, 86, 92

West, Asia and the, 24-25

Williams, Delores S., 25, 29

Wire, Antoinette, 50, 76

Woman, Syrophoenician, 71-83, 91-92; interpretation by Asian theologians, 81-82; Jesus and, 80; in Matthew and Mark, 73-75; Jesus and, 73-74; the Other and, 82-83; religious tra-

dition of, 81-82; Schüssler Fiorenza's reconstruction of story, 80-81; significations in story of, 74-75; Third World women and, 92

Women: African, 88; Asian, 47-49, 87; biblical, 93-94; Jesus and, xii-xvi, 78-79; Jewish, 89; Latin American, 88; meaning of term, 25-26; multiple identities of, 93-94; oppression of, 84, 87-88; role in creating scriptures, 45-49; silencing of, 52-53; Third World, 92; in view of missionaries, 78-79

Women and Jesus in Mark (Hisako Kinukawa), 80

World Council of Churches, seventh assembly (1991), 57, 70, 99

Writings, sacred, 92-93

Wu Yaozhong, 11

Yagi, Seiichi, 64

Yeo Khiok-khng, 61-62

Yuasa, Yuko, 65-66

Zhang Dongsun, 34

Zhao Zichen, 8, 10

Zionism, 98-99; the Bible and, 90